INDUSTRIAL CONSULTANCY

This book provides an in-depth analysis of industrial consultancy on a variety of issues and aspects including operations and services. This book:

- Looks at both individual-level consultancy and consultancy for firms, companies, or institutions.
- Uses observations, examples, and case studies to bring together key themes: consulting approach; production operations vs. services consulting; location and facilities criteria; human–machine interaction; lead time objective; outsourcing decisions and management; and infrastructure influence along with consultancy objectives, strategic considerations, and conflict resolution.
- Presents a comprehensive understanding of industrial consultancy and services offered to a wide range of industries, across type, size, and scale, including manufacturing, pharmaceutical, fabrication, and transformer industries.

The first of its kind, this book will be a useful resource for industry and management professionals as well as scholars and researchers of business management, business economics, operations, entrepreneurship and organizational behaviour, and engineering.

Sanjay Sharma is Professor at the National Institute of Industrial Engineering (NITIE), Mumbai, India. He is an industrial engineering and operations management educator and researcher with over three decades of experience in industry, management, teaching/training, consultancy, and research. A recipient of many awards and honours, he has published five books and papers in journals including the *European Journal of Operational Research, International Journal of Production Economics, Computers & Operations Research, International Journal of Advanced Manufacturing Technology, Journal of the Operational Research Society*, and *Computers and Industrial Engineering*. He is also a reviewer for several international journals and is on the editorial board of some journals including the *International Journal of Logistics Management*.

INDUSTRIAL CONSULTANCY

Operational Focus

Sanjay Sharma

Routledge
Taylor & Francis Group

LONDON AND NEW YORK

First published 2021
by Routledge
2 Park Square, Milton Park, Abingdon, Oxon OX14 4RN

and by Routledge
52 Vanderbilt Avenue, New York, NY 10017

Routledge is an imprint of the Taylor & Francis Group, an informa business

British Library Cataloguing-in-Publication Data
A catalogue record for this book is available from the British Library

Library of Congress Cataloging-in-Publication Data
A catalog record for this book has been requested

ISBN: 978-0-367-40896-1 (hbk)
ISBN: 978-0-367-41553-2 (pbk)
ISBN: 978-0-367-81519-6 (ebk)

Typeset in Sabon
by Apex CoVantage, LLC

CONTENTS

FIGURES

TABLES

PREFACE

With many scientific, technological, engineering, and management institutes taking an active interest in industrial consultancy, this book has emerged from a need for guidance in this area. It is expected to be highly useful to faculty of such institutes to get familiar with industrial consultancy. This book includes certain aspects of operations and services consulting, combining a general approach along with specific examples and cases. The contents of the book may not require an essential or strong engineering/scientific background; hence, it will prove to be helpful to readers from multiple disciplines. Lead time has been covered in detail along with interdepartmental conflicts. The book also includes location and facilities, productivity, and outsourcing considerations. Furthermore, it will be beneficial to consultancy organizations as a training resource for their new consultants in relevant areas. It will also be of interest to practitioners and postgraduate students of entrepreneurship in addition to engineering and management.

1

INTRODUCTION

Most of the available literature related to the area of consultancy covers management consultancy. This management consultancy is primarily related to strategic consulting, that is, inclusive of commercial/financial and also human resources aspects. Thus, there is a need for industrial consultancy literature with an operational focus. The existing literature pertaining to management/industrial consultancy focuses more on strategic planning activities before the actual start of industrial production and also services. However, the organizations deeply involved in manufacturing and also services, that is, those running the related business for a considerable period, also frequently require advice in order to improve their operational productivity. This book on industrial consultancy with an operational focus is an attempt to fill this gap.

Additionally, consulting firms recruit young professionals with postgraduate degrees in management as well as industrial engineering–related disciplines, among others. These professionals require a source of information when starting a career in industrial consultancy with the mentioned focus. This book is authored to address this requirement. Furthermore, many engineering and management institutions enter into industrial consultancy as time progresses; hence, associated faculty will find the book useful. This orientation will also help launch new elective courses for students in order to enhance their future prospects.

This book is organized into six chapters including this introductory chapter. As soon as one enters into an organization, the first thing that often comes to mind is location and also the manner in which the facilities are arranged in that place. Therefore, the second chapter addresses the location and facilities criteria. Once the resources are in place, the next question is how productive these are. Thus, the third chapter is related to the productivity consideration. An important next issue is how much time it takes for a finished industrial product to reach the customer after the order is received. The fourth chapter deals with this issue, that is, lead time objective. As outsourcing is a significant aspect of industrial/operational consulting, this is covered in the fifth chapter. Finally, a consultancy vision is provided in the last chapter.

The present chapter is concerned with some introductory details. Consultancy can be provided to any industrial or business organization, among others, on a variety of issues including operations and services. Consultancy might be offered at an individual level, as well as at a consultancy-providing firm or at an institutional level. It is shown in this chapter how consultancy can be offered at an individual level and at a company or an institutional level, explaining that industrial consultancy refers to the services offered to a variety of industries, irrespective of the type, size, and scale of the industries, and that such services might also be provided to any type of organization or for a specified time.

An individual depending on his or her qualifications and experience/expertise can offer the appropriate consulting services to the client or organization in need of such services. An individual or a team can also represent the institute or consultancy-providing firm. Whether this refers to a firm or individual, the consultancy can be offered to any organization including industrial.

Industrial consultancy might refer to a variety of industries. Some of these (also considering services) include the automobile industry, textile industry, pharmaceutical industry, IT industry, agricultural industry, and hotel/catering industry. Another classification for the industry depending on the investment/scale/size might be small industry, medium industry, or large industry.

Industrial consultancy refers to the related service provided to a company/organization in any kind of industry. However, such services might also be provided to any type of organization in general, including the services organization for a certain mutually agreed upon, specified time period.

A practitioner's approach is followed throughout this book using a simple style so that it is beneficial to the academic community, students, researchers, and teachers as well as professionals. The book has resulted entirely from my own industrial, managerial, and consulting experience of several years and hence is quite different from available literature, as is evident from the lack of many academic references on the subject. As a number of scientific, technological, engineering, and management institutes are taking an active interest in industrial consultancy, the growing need for such an approach is fulfilled. Many examples are included here in order to get an insight into industrial consultancy and to establish the usefulness of this emerging field.

1.1 Consulting approach

An interaction of the consultancy service provider or consultant and the organization desirous of availing such services is shown in Figure 1.1.

As mentioned before, a consultant may be an individual or a consultancy firm represented by one or more consultants. Either the organization may approach the consultant or the consultant may initiate the process in the form of marketing their services to the potential client.

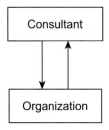

Figure 1.1 Interaction of a consultant and organization
Source: All figures and tables in this book are by the author.

1.1.1 *Organization-initiated process*

An industrial or business organization first of all realizes that certain external advice is needed for a particular issue. The organization-initiated process is shown in Figure 1.2.

First of all, the organization should ensure that there is an explicit need for availing the consultancy in a particular area. The need might be because of an attempt towards:

(i) Becoming competitive
(ii) Reorganization of activities

In order to approach a consultant/consulting firm, either informal or formal means may be adopted. Suppose that the organization had already hired a certain consultant/firm in the past, then they may be approached informally. Otherwise, the formal approach may be adopted, such as circulation of enquiry concerning the specified task. There may be a limited circulation inviting expression of interest among a few firms/individuals. In another situation, a wide publicity campaign might be planned at a national level or beyond. Either the whole task may be planned for assignment to the consultant in one go, or a component of the task might be planned initially. For example, the whole task may refer to:

Establishing standard time and manpower rationalization.

However, a component of the task (or subtask) may refer to:

Establishing standard time.

Table 1.1 shows a certain description related to the whole task/subtask assignment at a given time.

Since the whole task is composed of few subtasks, the time taken to complete the whole task is longer, along with a higher expected consultancy fee.

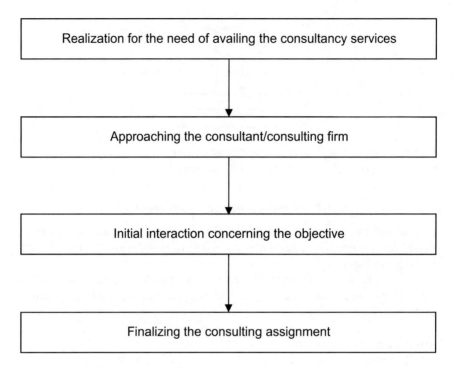

Figure 1.2 Organization-initiated process

Table 1.1 Whole task vs. subtask

Whole task assignment	Subtask assignment
Time taken by the consultant for completion is greater	Total time taken may be less
Greater consultancy fees	Fee may be comparatively less
Higher risk concerning satisfactory completion	Lower related risk
Better negotiation by the organization because of a larger investment	Comparatively less opportunity for negotiation

However, when expenditure of the organization is great, there are certain risks involved. In a case in which satisfactory completion of the assignment is not happening on time, it may not be a happy situation. At the same time, the client may be in a better position to negotiate concerning the amount of the consultancy fee before the finalization of the assignment to a particular consulting firm/consultant.

The initial interaction concerning the objective should include discussion pertaining to the scope of the work in addition to the desired task along with the associated fees. Irrespective of the whole task/subtask assignment, a considerable thinking process is needed regarding whether to obtain services for a particular section/department/area of the organization or throughout the organization. For example, if 'manpower rationalization' is to be done, the following might be options for an organization:

(i) To get it done first in a particular area such as 'manufacturing'.
(ii) To get it done throughout the organization including all the areas such as 'manufacturing', 'stores', and 'administration'.

Similarly, if a corporate organization has the three plants throughout the country, there is a need to consider whether the activity should be done first in one plant only or whether it should be done in all the plants and assigned to the consultant in one go. In the case in which the desired task/subtask is proposed to be done in one plant, the following are the concerned aspects:

(i) After observing the performance of a consultant at the time of completion of the task, a decision might be taken later to replicate the service in all the remaining plants. Risk may be lower. However, further efforts will be needed in terms of coordination, and a mutual agreement related to the fees and other conditions will be required.
(ii) In a case in which consultant performance is beyond doubt and an organization is also sure about the consultancy outcome in all the plants, the assignment for all the plants may happen in one go. This may avoid additional efforts concerning a fresh mutual agreement including a negotiation related to the fees and other relevant details.

After the initial interaction, the consulting assignment needs to be finalized. This should finally cover various aspects such as:

(i) Need for consultancy
(ii) Aim of the consultancy assignment
(iii) Approximate duration
(iv) Total fees along with other expenditure
(v) Resources needed
(vi) Implementation responsibility

Depending on the precise need, an explicit aim of the consultancy assignment should be documented. The mutually agreed upon document should also include an approximate expected duration in which the assignment has to be completed. Total fees are yet another aspect to be covered. It may also be mentioned whether a certain percentage of the total fees needs to be paid well in advance, that is, before the formal start of an assignment. Resources to be made available to the consultants (as and when needed) can also be mentioned, such as:

  (i) Suitable office space
 (ii) Computer system, printer, and stationery items
(iii) An experienced coordinator
(iv) Travelling arrangement
 (v) Secretarial assistance
(vi) Lodging and boarding

The type of secretarial assistance including the typing might be specified if it is needed. It needs to be mentioned whether the travelling arrangement will be made by the client or the consulting firm. An experienced coordinator may be deputed from the organization side, who will be a suitable link or a contact point between the client and the consultant.

In a case in which multiple consultants/firms express their interest in the intended assignment (Figure 1.3), the concerned organization has to decide in favour of the best option.

The following aspects might be helpful for a final selection:

  (i) Qualification and experience of the consultant
 (ii) Prior work done in a similar area
(iii) Reputation of the consulting firm/institute/individual consultant
(iv) Stated fees
 (v) Resources needed from the client organization
(vi) Current location of the consulting firm and its distance from the organization

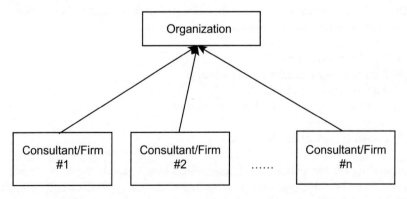

Figure 1.3 Expression of interest from multiple consultants/firms

(vii) Promised duration in which the assignment is supposed to be completed
(viii) How many visits of the consultant would be necessary and for how much time in each visit; also the number of consultants visiting the organization
(ix) Whether lodging and boarding will be arranged by the organization
(x) By whom the travelling expenses will be borne
(xi) Whether implementation of the final consultancy report will be the responsibility of an organization

1.1.2 Consultant-initiated process

Either an individual consultant or a representative of a consulting firm can also initiate the process. Initially the consultant may try to explore various organizations, as shown in Figure 1.4.

Depending on the case, these organizations may be companies in a similar sector/industry. For example, various companies in the pharmaceutical industry might be contacted. The companies may also belong to different sectors. For example, productivity improvement might be needed in the automobile industry as well as in the pharmaceutical industry. On the basis of initial information, such companies may be explored for developing suitable consulting assignments.

In order to gain considerable success in getting the assignment, a consultant should be able to convince the client organization that he or she is the suitable person to handle either the whole task or subtask. The consulting firm should also show that it has enough resources to undertake the intended assignment. For this, a first necessary step is the self-assessment, as shown in Figure 1.5, concerning the consultant-initiated process.

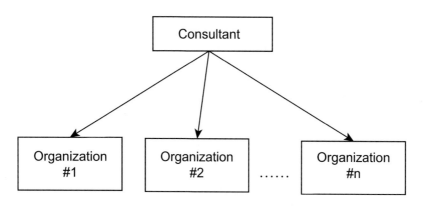

Figure 1.4 Exploring various organizations

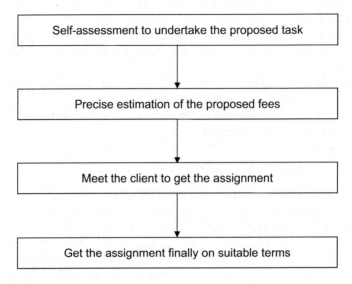

Figure 1.5 Consultant-initiated process

A self-assessment will reveal whether the consultant (or a consulting firm) has the requisite expertise to undertake the proposed task in terms of:

  (i) Qualifications
 (ii) Prior experience
(iii) Required necessary human resources
(iv) Required necessary computer packages/programmes
 (v) Necessary consultancy skills
(vi) Data generation
(vii) Report generation
(viii) Negotiation skills

After ensuring that the consultant is competent enough to approach the client organization, some initial relevant information may be gathered. In order to prepare the necessary proposal, an estimation of the fees to be charged should be made. Fees to be charged should be at a certain standard level, that is, neither too low nor too high. In the case of lower fees, the costs incurred by a consulting firm on resources including human resources may not be met appropriately. On the other hand, higher fees might lead to losing the assignment to competitors in that particular consulting area. Therefore, suitable competitive fees corresponding to the nature and amount of work should be estimated, and the client should be convinced regarding that. This will also help in underlining the sincere effort during the mutual discussion concerning the objective and duration of the consultancy assignment.

Table 1.2 Lower vs. higher fees

Lower fees	Higher fees
Client might be relatively happy to agree to such an arrangement in a brief amount of time.	Consultant might not get the assignment easily. The potential agreement, if any, might take a lot of time to finalize.
There may be a late realization for the consultant (after the start of assignment) that it is not viable/feasible.	Expectations of the client may be very high in terms of quality job/projected benefit.
Additional associated expenditure might not have been represented properly in the estimation of fees.	Possibility of an overestimation of the additional associated expenditure might affect competitiveness in the consultancy market.

Associated features of lower and higher fees are shown in Table 1.2, relatively. An appropriate relative comparison has been made available for the range of proposed fees, that is, lower/higher fees.

In order to meet with the client, certain preparation is necessary. The consultant should represent the self/consulting firm well in order to get the assignment. It is very necessary to convince the organization regarding:

(i) Required competence
(ii) Ability to complete the assignment in the required time
(iii) Ability to take the employees of the organization into confidence, in some cases, concerning the process and potential outcome of the consulting assignment
(iv) Fees are compatible with the nature of task/quality job

Finally, the consultant should try to get the assignment on suitable terms, or else it may lead to some dissatisfaction later. In a case in which negotiation is necessary, breakup of the task might be shared briefly along with the required total number of person-hours spent within the organization as well as outside. This may help in negotiation, along with developing confidence among the decision makers. Mutually agreed upon terms may include the following aspects suitably:

(i) When travelling, lodging, and boarding are to be arranged by the consultant, then such estimated expenses might be included in the total fees to be charged. Otherwise, the client organization may reimburse these expenses on the production of actual bills.
(ii) After submission of the final consultancy report to the satisfaction of the client, whether the responsibility for actual implementation will be that of the organization.

In many cases, the consultant may not be in a position to implement the recommendations throughout the organization. However, the consultant can make an effort to demonstrate the practicality and feasibility of implementation. Examples can be made available to the employees and management of the organization during the consultancy period. This may help with acceptance by management, and the organization may be able to take the responsibility for implementation of the recommendations throughout.

After discussing the approaches for initiating the consultancy process, certain strategic consideration would be helpful to the consultants in a broader understanding of the issues.

1.2 Strategic consideration

The aim of the consultancy might be at the business level or plant/technical level or micro level. However, in order to understand the position of a company/industry in the context of a national or global situation, a macro-level scenario may also be helpful. Such consideration may be useful for:

(i) Interaction of the global scenario and industry-level performance
(ii) Interaction of the national scenario and company-level performance
(iii) Comparison of two or more companies in a similar industry/sector
(iv) Learning from a different sector/industry
(v) Benchmarking

While considering the global situation and industry-level performance concerned with a nation, appropriate parameters must be found for suitable analysis. Depending on the company or sector, such parameters can be, for example, regarding:

(i) Export situation
(ii) Import criteria
(iii) Production/productivity
(iv) Quality/substitution of materials
(v) Design/development
(vi) Supply of input items

In the case of the export-import, a global export level should be understood. After knowing a few competing nations in that business, the export share of each in the context of total value should be considered. This will give an idea of where a particular sector of the country under consideration stands. The next step should be to learn the reasons for a higher share in the global export level. Reasons for a higher share might include:

(i) Competitive price

(ii) Good-quality product

(iii) Desired input item used for the finally manufactured product

(iv) Shorter total lead time

(v) Low domestic demand

(vi) Favourable currency scenario

(vii) Government policy

Similarly, the reasons for a higher import level in a country under consideration can be found if that is needed. This might happen when domestic demand is so high that it cannot be fulfilled by the local producers. Such reasons can pave the way for suitable strategic advice in order to improve the performance of the sector as a whole in a particular nation. Figure 1.6 shows the link among the global scenario with the sector and individual company in a particular sector. Strategic decision/proposals may be considered by the government also at the sector level. Such aspects also directly or indirectly influence advice from the consulting firm, as the strategic or macro-level scenario affects the sector. And, in turn, an individual organization/company may also be advised strategically as well as at a micro or operational level.

Any relevant parameter in general can be analyzed at various levels including the global, and certain insights can be generated. For instance, the global benchmark can be linked to other levels concerning the parameters such as productivity and quality. Similarly, a benchmark may be related to design/development. In certain situations, a particular item (that goes into a final product) may play a role in the export scenario/an increase in demand. In

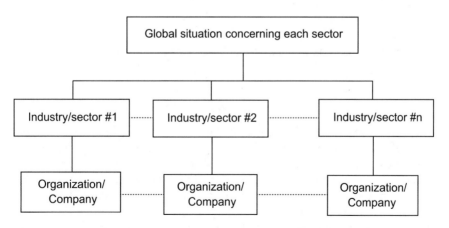

Figure 1.6 Linking global scenario with an industry and company

this way, the procurement strategy of an input item at an organization level may be advised using the discussed link.

The mentioned analysis is also useful for comparing two or more companies in a similar sector and also benchmarking those. Although the different industrial/business sectors are analyzed separately, there is a chance for learning among the different sectors. For example, a procurement/supply chain strategy of one type of industry can be adopted by another sector for their own nature of operations if it appears to be beneficial.

1.3 Production operations vs. services consulting

The operations are traditionally associated with production operations, some of which are as follows:

(i) Manufacturing
(ii) Chemical processing
(iii) Textile
(iv) Product assembly

On the other hand, the services sector may include:

(i) Banking
(ii) Administrative
(iii) Educational
(iv) Hospitals

However, both these types broadly can also be written as:

(i) Production operations
(ii) Service operations

Conventional production operations vs. service operations are summarized in Table 1.3.

1.3.1 Production operations

Focus is more on the facilities, as shown in Figure 1.7. Although the arrangement of facilities is of different varieties, typical arrangement is depicted.

Raw material enters towards the facilities for the different production processes, and a finished product is available after the last facility process. Movement of the material is analyzed, and the suggestions may be provided to add or reduce the number of similar facilities in a line. In certain cases, material handling and the associated cost might be of significance. Quality of the raw material and finished product, and the effects, can be examined.

12

Table 1.3 Production vs. service operations

Production	Services
Focus is more on the facilities	Focus is more on the human resources
Movement of the material is analyzed	Movement of the human being can be observed
Material handling might be important	Handling the public might be significant
Corporate profitability is given due significance in the production operations	Commercial viability may take a back seat in certain cases when a public service is given due importance
Maintenance of a large number of facilities may be a costly affair	Maintenance of a relatively small number of facilities in some cases may not be that problematic
Raw material quality and the manufactured product quality are maintained	An effort should be made to improve the service quality

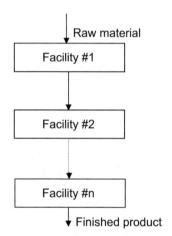

Figure 1.7 Various facilities

Because of a large number of facilities, a maintenance procedure and its standardization might be some issues, among others. Production operations are set up with a certain investment, and it is very important to link the activities with corporate profitability.

1.3.2 Service operations

Focus is more on the human resources, as shown in Figure 1.8 concerning a service counter, for example. The service counter might relate to a bank, such as a cash transaction counter.

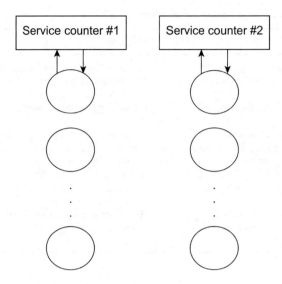

Figure 1.8 Queue before the service counter

In the case of a hospital, patient movement as well as the doctors' movement should be observed, and modifications should be made accordingly. For example, a public service and handling the public are given due importance in government hospitals as compared to commercial viability.

In some cases, the maintenance of a relatively small number of facilities may not be so problematic. However, the service quality needs to be improved, for instance, in the case of an 'after-sale service' in the corporate sector also.

Although some of the characteristics may be different concerning production and service operations, most of the practical business situations are exhibited both within the same organization. For example, the basic activity of the manufacturing organization is the production operation. However, many supporting services coexist, such as the accounts and administration. On the production shop floor also, there is a significant interaction of the facilities and human resources. Similarly, a movement of the materials as well as human resources happens simultaneously. For providing consultancy in operations and services, it is necessary to know the variety of consultancy objectives.

1.4 Consultancy objectives

In order to understand a wide variety of consultancy objectives, some different examples are provided here.

Example 1.1

A pharmaceutical company has a few production divisions for medicines. After mixing of the input materials, such as powder/compound, these are processed and packaged. A few production and packaging lines are available in each division. Currently, the company runs in all three shifts. However, the output of these shifts differ considerably. It is decided by the management to go for a manpower productivity improvement and the rationalization of manpower. In addition to the production division, there are other relevant areas such as:

(i) Raw material store
(ii) Quality control
(iii) Utilities
(iv) Packaged medicine storage

Productivity improvement is needed throughout the company, including the associated services.

Example 1.2

A transformer manufacturing company designs and manufactures transformers of various specifications. The customers include power generation and distribution companies in the public and private sectors. Various state electricity boards also procure the transformers. Currently, most of the transformers take three to five months to design, manufacture, and dispatch. However, the management feels that the total lead time is on the longer side, and there is enough scope for reducing the overall lead time. In order to achieve this significant consultancy objective, the following activities are proposed to be considered:

(i) Design of the transformer
(ii) Approval of the design and drawing
(iii) Procurement of the input materials
(iv) Winding for the transformers
(v) Subsequent processes and subassemblies
(vi) Final assembly
(vii) Suitable packaging and dispatch

Additionally, there is a role for the following functions:

(i) Production planning and control, in the context of providing an overall plan for the machine loading and also workers on the shop floor
(ii) Quality testing and inspection at various stages of the transformer manufacturing and assembly

Example 1.3

An old steel rolling mill is spread out in a large area, and the arrangement of various departments may not be appropriate. It is also felt by the management that their competitiveness in comparison with the relatively new rolling mills has been lost. A significant reason for this is attributed to the overall plant layout, and because of that the total material handling cost is quite high. In order to become competitive, a change in layout is a major consultancy objective. This can be achieved by way of material flow analysis and the suggested changes in plant layout that are practically suitable.

In a case in which a certain investment is needed in shifting the machines and departments, a suitable cost-benefit analysis may be provided.

Example 1.4

In the case of pressure vessel fabrication, a new test has been suggested by the relevant bureau for developing standards. The factory needs to design and develop it in order to fulfill the requirement concerning relevant standards. It is expected that this might take approximately two months. As the regular employees are busy with day-to-day production and other related activities, it is decided to outsource this task to an external consultant with the expectations as follows:

(i) Study of the existing standards, particularly the newly introduced test
(ii) In order to develop a testing facility in the factory, suitable design of the apparatus and the related features would be necessary
(iii) Procurement of the necessary materials
(iv) Machining process to make the items suitable for assembly
(v) Installation and the demonstration of a successful testing procedure

Example 1.5

The World Bank (in association with the concerned government) may need a suitable consultancy organization for their project related to procuring and supplying various items to government schools in certain countries. This objective may require the following activities to be fulfilled by a potential consultancy organization:

(i) Prepare the detailed specifications (along with the drawing where necessary) for the intended items
(ii) Release of the global tender
(iii) Tender analysis (an appropriate cost estimation is also to be made in order to compare the quotation offered)
(iv) Selection of the suitable suppliers

(v) Necessary approval of the stakeholders at various stages
(vi) Quality inspection before dispatching the items to various schools

Example 1.6

A container and freight forwarding agency has a fleet of approximately one hundred trucks and also employs a similar number of drivers. Thus, there is almost one-to-one correspondence concerning the truck and driver. The company forwards containers to the dock, after stuffing the container with the goods to be exported. The trucks will carry these filled and sealed containers to the dock for shipping them to the destination.

Similarly, the trucks carry the imported goods containers from the dock to a company warehouse. After de-stuffing the goods, those are received by the customers/dispatched to the customers or stored in the warehouse temporarily. In order to improve the overall productivity of their operations, the consultancy objective includes various subobjectives, such as:

(i) Critical analysis of the activities that incorporate the stuffing and de-stuffing of containers and subsequent suggestions for improvement and standardization
(ii) Observation concerning maintenance practices of the trucks and recommendations
(iii) Overall reduction in the time taken by the trucks on the road considering the journey between the company and the dock (to and fro)
(iv) Analysis related to the time taken by a truck within the company premises for the de-stuffing/stuffing and necessary paperwork

Example 1.7

In a chemical process factory, it is felt that energy plays a significant role and the energy consumption throughout the factory should be analyzed. An appropriate consultancy objective can be energy auditing. For the purpose of energy auditing, it is necessary to know:

(i) In a suitable specified period, how much is the total power consumption?
(ii) How much power is consumed department-/section-wise?
(iii) Depending on a large share concerning energy consumption, which department should be paid specific attention? Similarly, in the processes, which facilities are responsible for greater power consumption, so that the special focus can be related to those facilities for improvement in this area?
(iv) How much power is purchased from an external source, and how much is the captive power generation?
(v) What are the opportunities for energy savings and appropriate recommendations in this area?

Example 1.8

A newspaper publishing/printing company may have their activities critically analyzed and get suggestions for improvement. It involves some of these activities:

(i) Printing machine setup for a variety of matter appearing in the newspaper
(ii) Scheduling/sequencing for different matter
(iii) Time lag between arrival of information and actual printing

Additionally, some of their customers/readers get the newspapers not on conventional time, but there is some delay. What are the reasons behind this delay?

This requires a critical observation after the bundles of newspapers leave the publishing house, that is, the start of delivery van until the doorstep of the actual readers/end customers.

Example 1.9

A logistics service provider wants to invest in the modernization of areas such as:

(i) Customer order receiving process
(ii) Management of a fleet of vehicles
(iii) Warehousing

In the event of a limited budget, it is necessary to prioritize the areas/activities. In order to achieve this objective, an approach might be as follows:

(i) Estimate the desirable investment in each area for modernization.
(ii) How much is the payback period for each respective area?
(iii) What is the activity needing immediate attention and also having potential for the business growth in a short term?
(iv) Depending on the limited budget, prioritize the area considering the relevant information and analytical effort.

Example 1.10

Material flow analysis is helpful for an ease in handling the product/material or enhancing the flow speed. In case of the L.P.G. cylinder fabrication industry, a variety of tests are conducted for the purpose of quality inspection. When production volume is not that much or considerable, one testing line related to the hydrostatic stretch test for L.P.G. cylinders may exist. On rollers, the fabricated L.P.G. cylinders can enter from one side. The facility having an arrangement for filling water in the cylinder and then increasing the pressure inside the cylinder can appear on the top and side. It is to be observed whether there is any leakage from the cylinder. Then the cylinder can make an exit from the other side on rollers and finally be unloaded from such a facility.

When production volume becomes higher, two testing facilities may be needed. For this purpose, a variety of arrangements are possible. A suitable arrangement needs to be finalized after the study of:

(i) Number of workers needed for handling the cylinders at entry and exit concerning the facilities
(ii) Balancing the material flow and an ease in handling with a lower requirement of workers

Example 1.11

After the L.P.G. cylinder is completely fabricated, the following tests among others are conducted:

(i) Pre-pneumatic test
(ii) Final pneumatic test

In these pneumatic tests, the compressed air is filled in the cylinder and then the cylinder is dipped in a water tank. The test is done to check any leakage of air in the form of bubbles in the water-filled tank. After the pre-pneumatic test, the following processes take place:

(i) Shot blasting
(ii) Metallizing
(iii) Primer coating
(iv) Final painting
(v) Valve fitting

Then the final pneumatic test is carried out for any potential leakage including that from the valve also.

Third-party inspection is necessary at certain stages before and after pre-pneumatic tests, such as after metallizing. For the pre-pneumatic as well as final pneumatic tests, one inspector and two workers are traditionally deployed from the organization side. Two different teams of one inspector and two workers each currently exist. After a study of certain aspects, an objective is to explore the possibility of similar teams, that is, one team for both kinds of pneumatic tests and thus a manpower productivity improvement.

Example 1.12

In the case of a large retailer, the consumers pick the retail items. After picking, these consumers bring the items to the billing facility with the bar code reader. Certain space is often convenient to keep the items at the inlet side.

At the inlet side, consumers often place the items one after another from the trolley. At each billing facility, two employees are often available. One person takes each item to the bar code reader and as it is entered into the system, the items are transferred to the adjacent space for putting the items in a suitable bag by another person. After the bill generation and payment, the consumers can take the bags filled with their purchased items at the outlet side.

It has been observed that many customers have to wait for longer time at inlet sides of the billing facilities. In order to reduce the waiting time and congestion, various options have to be explored and suitable option needs to be implemented.

Example 1.13

A steel tube manufacturing company produces the tube/pipe in a variety of:

(i) Diameters
(ii) Thicknesses
(iii) Lengths

The immediate input item is the cold rolled coil for certain products. The coils are slit into a suitable width, and the appropriate width of the coil is formed into pipe or tube and finally welded and cut to a suitable length. The mentioned input item, that is, those coils, can be procured from outside. However, there is considerable distance between the major supplier company and the buyer, that is, the steel tube manufacturing company. Because of this, the transportation cost is higher. Depending on the thickness of the final product, that is, the steel tube, a wide variety of thicknesses for the coil is needed. Different alternatives need to be analyzed thoroughly such as the following:

(a) Procure a wide variety of thicknesses of coils and directly take the coils to a tube mill as input items.
(b) Procure a very small variety of thicknesses of coils and introduce an intermediate operation for reducing the thickness to the precise need of steel tube.

A few consultancy objectives have been mentioned. If the specific objective is stated in the mutually agreed upon document, it helps a lot in getting the final consultancy report approved by the client. Along with the objective, the precise methodology may also be mentioned in order to avoid any potential conflict while following the stated method. This may consist of brief details regarding:

(i) Data collection
(ii) Needed equipment, if any, for recording the observation
(iii) Frequency of sharing the outcome in the whole period

(iv) Interaction with the employees

(v) Level of management involved in frequently sharing the outcome

(vi) Authority for a final approval of the consultancy report recommendations and final release of the payment to the consultancy organization

In the present introductory chapter, a consulting approach has been described in detail. Along with the strategic consideration, production operations vs. service operations have been explained. Also a wide variety of consultancy objectives have been provided.

There are opportunities to decide in favour of a certain location and the particular facility planning issues from a wide variety of options. The second chapter deals with the various practical considerations for an industrial location. Different examples are considered for a material flow analysis, along with the layout. These include material handling efforts and other factors. A systematic approach is provided to initiate a consultancy in this area supported by the relevant table for data collection and subsequent analysis. This has also been illustrated by a steel rolling mill example, along with the significance of layout in their production and material flow.

While considering the productivity at an organization level, two factors are usually taken into account in general, that is, an output level and an input criterion. Several combinations of output and input variation in general are discussed in the third chapter. Manpower productivity has been specifically described including a standard approach along with cases such as the L.P.G. cylinder manufacturing industry and pharmaceutical industry. The role of manpower in such industries is narrated along with ways to improve the productivity in terms of either an increase in output or a decrease in input. This also includes the human–machine interaction specifically and its effects. Energy auditing in these industries, among others, is a useful first step to energy saving that can also be a unique measure for the productivity consideration. Various aspects have also been explained in the context of benchmarking.

Lead time is the time span between the point of time when actual services are performed and that when an order was placed for services. It can be associated with service as well as production operations. The role of lead time is explained thoroughly in production and associated service operations in the fourth chapter. Numerous examples and cases have been provided for a wide variety of industries, such as fabrication. Also included are an existing lead time analysis and its reduction. An exhaustive case has been included considering the transformer manufacturing industry. Additionally, different types of interactions have been described. The management should pay attention to sort out the differences of opinions and objectives, and an effort should be made to eliminate or reduce the interdepartmental conflicts presently found in the organization.

If certain activities including products or services are sourced from outside, then it is termed outsourcing. Basics of outsourcing are discussed, including cost as well as non-cost factors, in the fifth chapter. Associated costs while insourcing and outsourcing have been compared to make a suitable decision. Cases are mentioned considering the steel tube production and L.P.G. cylinder manufacturing industry. The outsourcing relationship between buyer and supplier is described specifically, including the factors influencing it. Service operations are also provided, such as an after-sale service along with its effect. Outsourcing management needs immediate attention in order to enhance the probability of success while outsourcing. Important aspects pertaining to this are narrated to make a suitable example.

The last chapter in this book applies a futuristic approach for projecting the vision of consultancy. This covers the role of technology in various production and service operations. The influence of infrastructure on various factors and the choices has been specifically introduced in order to improve efficiency/productivity, among other objectives. Channel design associated with production and services, including logistics, has been envisioned for introducing further efficiency in industrial/business functions. The need concerning additional attention for a holistic view has been emphasized.

Exercises

1 Discuss various levels at which a consultancy can be offered.
2 Explain different opportunities for providing an industrial consultancy to the following types of sectors:

   (i) Automobile industry
   (ii) Textile industry
   (iii) Pharmaceutical industry
   (iv) IT industry
   (v) Agricultural industry
   (vi) Hotel/catering industry

3 Describe the challenges faced in order to offer a consultancy to the following:

   (i) Small industry
   (ii) Medium industry
   (iii) Large industry

4 In the context of an organization-initiated process, elaborate the following issues:

   (i) Realization of the need of availing the consultancy services
   (ii) Approaching the consultant/consulting firm
   (iii) Initial interaction concerning the objective
   (iv) Finalizing the consulting assignment

5 Provide, with the help of a table, a certain description related to the whole task/subtask assignment at a given time.

6 In order to finalize the consulting assignment, elaborate the following issues:

    (i) Need for consultancy
    (ii) Aim of the consultancy assignment
    (iii) Approximate duration
    (iv) Total fees along with other expenditures
    (v) Resources needed
    (vi) Implementation responsibility

7 In the context of resources to be made available to the consultants, discuss the following:

    (i) Suitable office space
    (ii) Computer system, printer, and stationery items
    (iii) An experienced coordinator
    (iv) Travelling arrangements
    (v) Secretarial assistance
    (vi) Lodging and boarding

8 Discuss the expression of interest from multiple consultants/firms considering the following illustration:

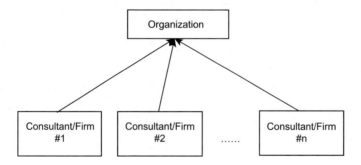

9 Describe the process of exploring various organizations considering the following illustration:

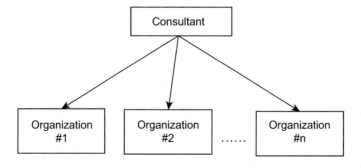

10 In the context of a consultant-initiated process, elaborate the following aspects:

(i) Self-assessment to undertake the proposed task
(ii) Precise estimation for the proposed fees
(iii) Meeting the client to get the assignment
(iv) Get the assignment finally on suitable terms

11 Discuss lower vs. higher fees with the help of a table.

12 Explain why it is very necessary to convince the organization regarding:

(i) Required competence
(ii) Ability to complete the assignment in the required time
(iii) Ability to take the employees of the organization into confidence in some cases concerning the process and potential outcome of the consulting assignment
(iv) Fees being compatible with the nature of task/quality job

13 In order to understand the position of a company/industry in the context of a national or global situation, a macro-level scenario may be helpful. Discuss how such a consideration may be useful for:

(i) Interaction of the global scenario and industry-level performance
(ii) Interaction of the national scenario and company-level performance
(iii) Comparison of two or more companies in a similar industry/sector
(iv) Learning from the different sector/industry
(v) Benchmarking

14 While considering the global situation and industry-level performance concerned with a nation, appropriate parameters must be found for a suitable analysis. Depending on the company or sector, explain how such parameters can be regarding:

(i) Export situation
(ii) Import criteria
(iii) Production/productivity
(iv) Quality/substitution of materials
(v) Design/development
(vi) Supply of input items

15 After knowing a few competing nations in a business, export share of each in the context of total value should be considered. This gives an idea where a particular sector of the country under consideration stands. The next step should be to determine the reasons for a higher share in the global export. Describe how the reasons for a higher share might include:

(i) Competitive price
(ii) Good-quality product
(iii) Desired input item used for the finally manufactured product

(iv) Shorter total lead time
(v) Low domestic demand
(vi) Favourable currency scenario
(vii) Government policy

16 Elaborate how one can link the global scenario with the industry and company considering the illustration as follows:

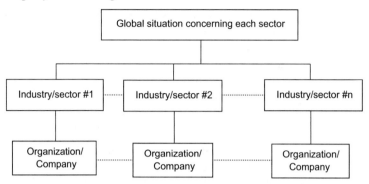

17 Describe production operations with reference to:

(i) Manufacturing
(ii) Chemical processing
(iii) Textiles
(iv) Product assembly

18 Discuss service operations with reference to:

(i) Banking
(ii) Administrative
(iii) Educational
(iv) Hospitals

19 Summarize production vs. service operations in a tabular form.
20 Explain the problems of production operations considering the typical arrangement of facilities as given here:

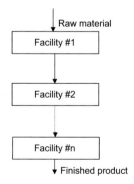

21 The World Bank (in association with the concerned government) may need a suitable consultancy organization for their project related to procuring and supplying various items to government schools in certain countries. Explain a suitable approach for such an objective that may require the following activities to be fulfilled by a potential consultancy organization:

  (i) Prepare the detailed specifications (along with a drawing where necessary) for the intended items
  (ii) Release of the global tender
  (iii) Tender analysis (an appropriate cost estimation is also to be made in order to compare the quotation offered)
  (iv) Selection of suitable suppliers
  (v) Necessary approval of the stakeholders at various stages
  (vi) Quality inspection before dispatching the items to various schools

22 A newspaper publishing/printing company may have their activities critically analyzed and get suggestions for improvement. This involves some of the activities within the house. Additionally, some of their customers/readers get the newspapers not on conventional time, but with some delay. In order to determine the reasons behind this delay, provide a suitable approach. This requires critical observation after the bundles of newspapers leave the publishing house, that is, the start of delivery van until the doorstep of the actual readers/end customers.

23 Explain the problems of service operations in a wide variety of contexts with inclusion of the queue, considering the illustration as follows:

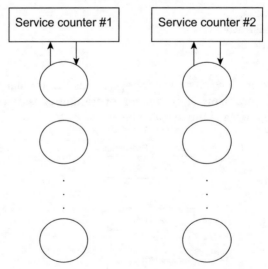

24 A logistics service provider wants to invest in the modernization of areas such as:

(i) Customer order receiving process

(ii) Management of a fleet of vehicles

(iii) Warehousing

In the event of a limited budget, it is necessary to prioritize the areas/activities on which to focus. In order to achieve this objective, comment on the following aspects:

(i) Estimate the desirable investment in each area for modernization.

(ii) How much is the payback period for each respective area?

(iii) What is the activity needing immediate attention and also having potential for business growth in the short term?

(iv) Depending on the limited budget, prioritize the area on which to focus, considering relevant information and an analytical effort.

25 Consider the following situation:

In the case of pressure vessel fabrication, a new test has been suggested by the relevant bureau for developing standards. The factory needs to design and develop it in order to fulfill the requirement concerning relevant standards. It is expected that this might take approximately two months. As the regular employees are busy with day-to-day production and other related activities, it is decided to outsource this task to the external consultant with expectations as follows:

(i) Study of the existing standards, particularly the newly introduced test

(ii) In order to develop a testing facility in the factory, a suitable design of the apparatus and related features would be necessary

(iii) Procurement of the necessary materials

(iv) Machining to make the items suitable for assembly

(v) Installation and demonstration for a successful testing procedure

In view of these expectations, provide an approach to undertake such tasks. Also comment on the following:

(i) Advantages of insourcing this task

(ii) Disadvantages of insourcing this task

(iii) Benefits of outsourcing such an objective

(iv) Problems of outsourcing such an objective

(v) Estimation of time to complete this job

(vi) Resources needed

(vii) Need for subcontracting a certain portion of the whole task

(viii) Implementation responsibility

(ix) Involvement of internal resources

(x) Factors affecting the consulting fees

(xi) Adoption of the testing procedure by stakeholders

2

LOCATION AND FACILITIES CRITERIA

A basic and primary factor is location of an organization in general. Also, the layout in that location significantly impacts organizational processes. This chapter covers such aspects in detail in order to provide sufficient background to the reader. This background helps in the overall context of design and productivity of such resources. Many old plants need suitable advice in order to improve their layout for smooth material flow. A systematic approach is provided to initiate a consultancy in this area supported by relevant tables for data collection and subsequent analysis. This has also been illustrated by a steel rolling mill example, along with the significance of layout in their production and material flow.

A suitable location where an industrialist/entrepreneur can start business activities is of utmost importance. Usually, advice might be sought on this issue first, and then the need for facilities arrangement may be focused on. The location and facilities criteria have operational as well as strategic significance. These aspects are emphasized from the point of view of industrial consultancy with a reasonable practical approach.

In order to locate an industrial or business organization, a few points should be taken into consideration first. These include whether the end consumer interaction is direct or whether the end consumer interaction is indirect.

After deciding about the location, various facilities are established in that location, keeping in mind the different objectives such as line balancing, space utilization, smooth material handling, material handling cost minimization, material storage, and also the convenience for logistics.

However, the first decision to be made is about the location, that is, where to establish a production or service organization.

2.1 Location consideration

If a consultant has been asked to help in deciding about a location, then immediate attention should go to the type of organization, that is, whether it is based on production or services. In the case of production activity, an

28

end consumer interaction is usually indirect, that is, through dealers and retailers. However, in the case of services, the end consumer interaction is usually direct. In certain cases, the consumer–company interaction becomes relevant instead of the end consumer interaction. Therefore, a discussion can happen with a focus on:

(i) End consumer interaction
(ii) Consumer–company interaction

2.1.1 End consumer interaction

For a generalization, Figure 2.1 is useful, with a focus on the end consumer interaction.

Considering the organization type, that is, production or services, and the interaction with the end customer, the various related categories are I, II, III, and IV. Categories I and II relate to the production organization, and categories III and IV relate to the service organization. An end consumer interaction is direct in the case of categories II and III, whereas it is indirect in the case of categories I and IV. These categories are discussed next.

I

This is the usual case in which a production organization has an indirect interaction with the end consumer, as depicted in Figure 2.2.

The general characteristic features of category I are shown in Table 2.1 in the context of a location consideration.

The following are the possibilities for a location consideration:

(i) Near end consumer
(ii) Away from the end consumer

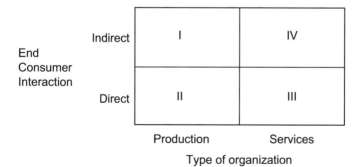

Figure 2.1 End consumer interaction

29

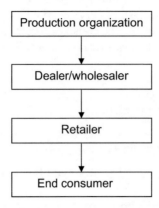

Figure 2.2 Indirect interaction of production with end consumer

Table 2.1 Characteristics of category I

Near end consumer	*Away from end consumer*
Costly location	Possibility of a cheaper location
Higher fixed cost	Lower fixed cost
Larger area may not be available	Availability of larger area
Costly storage area	Less costly storage area
Lower transportation cost to consumers	Higher transportation cost to consumers

If a location is nearer to the final customers, that is, where the number of such customers is greater, then there is a possibility of costly location in terms of a purchase price. This is because of a densely populated and also most probably a commercial area. A higher fixed cost is incurred owing to this reason. In such locations, a larger area may not be available. Or if, in the rare case, it is available, the cost factor is prohibitive. In many situations, a certain storage area for finished products is necessary at the outlet of a production plant or nearer that, thus a costly storage area. However, since the location is nearer to the end customers, the transportation cost is lower to take the goods to the consumers.

In a case in which a location is away from the final customers, a cheaper location may be available in terms of the purchase price and a lower fixed cost is incurred because of this reason. A larger area may be available and can be purchased also due to a favourable cost. This additional area may be used for expansion purposes in the future. The storage area for finished items may also be arranged because it is less costly. As the end consumers are away from the production plant, a higher transportation cost is needed in order to take the goods to consumers.

II

Although it may not be usual, in certain cases, a production organization may like to have a direct interaction with the end consumer, as shown in Figure 2.3.

In comparison with the previous category, an additional factor might be considered, that is, lead time. The lead time is the difference between the point of time when a consumer gets the desired product and the point of time when that consumer expresses his or her desire to buy the product formally. If the location for such an organization is near the end consumer, a shorter lead time is expected. In a case in which the location is far away from the end consumer, a longer lead time may be proposed. Among other factors, the location consideration may analyze:

(i) Fixed cost
(ii) Transportation cost
(iii) Lead time

The general characteristic features of category II are shown in Table 2.2 in the context of location consideration.

In the previous category, a general choice may be to establish the production plant away from an end consumer. This is because dealers/retailers might store the items and lead time may not be that relevant for a production facility having no direct interaction with the consumers. However, in the present category, a general choice may be to establish a production plant near the end consumers if it is feasible. In this case, a higher fixed cost is offset by a lower transportation cost and the potential advantages of a shorter lead time. Furthermore, this is possible only when environmental regulations permit such an establishment near the end consumers.

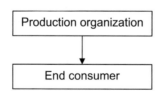

Figure 2.3 Direct interaction of production with end consumer

Table 2.2 Characteristics of category II

Away from end consumer	Near end consumer
Lower fixed cost	Higher fixed cost
Higher transportation cost	Lower transportation cost
Longer lead time	Shorter lead time

III

This is the usual case, as shown in Figure 2.4, since most services have a direct interaction with the end consumers.

Such service organizations therefore can have their setup nearer to the consumers as a preferred choice. Generally, a larger area may not be needed as compared to a production facility setup, and thus a fixed cost implication is relatively less.

IV

Although it may be unusual, certain services may not have direct interaction with end consumers. For instance, cleanliness services may have a direct interaction with citizens; however, maintenance of the garbage trucks and other equipment may not have a direct relevance for them. There might be a possibility to have major maintenance activities away (as shown in Figure 2.5) from the main city, depending on various other factors and constraints. Such factors and constraints may relate to the availability of space and traffic congestion among others.

End consumer interaction has been discussed in detail along with various categories, that is, I, II, III, and IV, in the context of production or manufacturing as well as services to customers. However, there are cases in which a consumer–company interaction becomes more relevant.

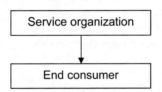

Figure 2.4 Direct interaction of services with end consumer

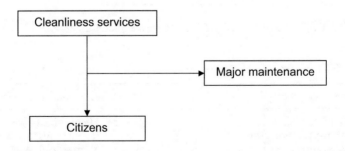

Figure 2.5 Indirect relevance of major maintenance activities

2.1.2 Consumer–company interaction

In services as well as production, a business organization may deal with another business or industrial organization. For example, an information technology firm may provide services to another organization either within the country or outside. Similarly, in manufacturing such cases have been observed.

Example 2.1

As shown in Figure 2.6, an L.P.G. cylinder manufacturing company does not have direct interaction with end consumers.

A cylinder manufacturing company produces empty cylinders, and those are supplied to an oil company. The oil company then fills the gas in cylinders at its filling plant, and then the filled cylinders reach the dealers' locations. Through the dealers, L.P.G. cylinders reach the end consumers. In a way, it appears like category I, discussed in the previous section. However, there is a certain difference.

After handing over the empty cylinders to an oil company, the role of the manufacturing company ends. After filling the gas in empty cylinders at the filling plant of an oil company satisfactorily, the cylinder becomes the property of the concerned oil company, and furthermore distribution happens through dealers to the end users. In such a case, proximity to the consumer company, that is, the filling plant of an oil company, becomes relevant, as shown in Figure 2.7.

In the present case, one cylinder production company exists nearer the filling plant. However, another production company has chosen to locate their facilities relatively away from the filling plant. The fixed cost of the

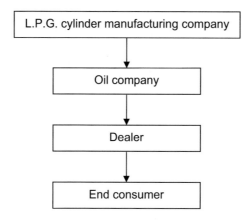

Figure 2.6 Indirect interaction with consumers in an L.P.G. business

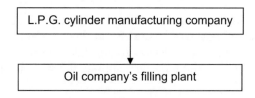

Figure 2.7 Interaction with the consumer company

first production company is comparatively higher on account of the location, but it can take the advantage of a lower transportation cost to the consumer company's filling plant. The related transportation cost in the case of the second production company is higher, but the fixed cost is lower. Furthermore, they have purchased a larger area for expansion purposes also. Because of a lower fixed cost, their breakeven point is also lower.

It has been observed that a fluctuating demand for empty L.P.G. cylinders also exists. It is a matter of concern when the fluctuating demand is on the lower side. This is because of reasons such as:

(i) Filling plant capacity
(ii) Reuse of the cylinders
(iii) Focus of the oil company on other products

Other products such as aviation fuel and automobile fuel, including petrol and diesel, are also important segments for the oil company business. Furthermore, because of a higher profit margin, their interest might be more towards such products in comparison with the L.P.G. business.

As discussed earlier, the breakeven point is lower in case of the second L.P.G. cylinder manufacturing company due to a lower fixed cost on account of the location choice. In the event of fluctuating demand, particularly on the lower side due to filling plant capacity among other reasons, this company can still maintain the breakeven point/profitability.

Since this company purchased a larger area for expansion purposes, they can also enter into production of relatively small cylinders, utilizing the available area for storage purposes among other things. These smaller cylinders can be easily carried from one place to another, that is, they are more suitable from portability point of view, and there is a customer segment for such cylinders. If the company wishes to do so, it might be relatively easier to enter into this activity.

The available larger area also has enough open space. This can additionally be utilized for certain operations on used cylinders. As shown in Figure 2.8, the consumer company, that is, the oil company, can send the used cylinders periodically to the manufacturing company for minor/major repair.

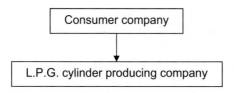

Figure 2.8 Reverse journey of used cylinders

The first operation is degassing the used cylinders, as those might carry small amounts of gas. It is preferred to do this operation in an open space as far as possible. This also presents an important locational advantage for the manufacturing company. Depending on minor/major repair, a certain sequence of operations are to be carried out after degassing. In cases in which only small dents are visible on the cylinder body, these can be rectified. Similarly, if only paint has worn out, surface finishing such as painting can be done. For these issues, surface finishing and testing such as leakage testing would be enough. However, dealing with the following defects/issues would come under major rework/repair, such as:

(i) Foot ring, which gives support to the cylinder kept on the floor, is damaged and needs to be replaced.
(ii) Valve protection ring, which is used for ease in handling and also protects the valve during handling, is damaged and needs to be replaced.

Since a welding operation is required in these cases, heat treatment and subsequent operations are necessary to conduct. As the damaged foot ring/valve protection ring is removed and then the new ring is welded to the cylinder body, residual stresses are developed, and for stress relieving, heat treatment is done. The subsequent operations/tests include:

(i) Hydrostatic stretch testing
(ii) Pre-pneumatic testing
(iii) Shot blasting
(iv) Metallizing
(v) Primer coating
(vi) Final painting
(vii) Valve fitting and final pneumatic test

After repair/rework, these cylinders are to be sent back to the consumer company, that is, the filling plant of the oil company, as shown in Figure 2.9, so that these are ready for filling the liquefied petroleum gas and further use.

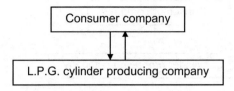

Figure 2.9 To-and-fro journey of used cylinders

A certain locational advantage has been discussed in the present example in terms of ease of entering into additional business processes, among others.

All the advantages may not be available in a particular location; however, the following aspects may be considered in general:

(i) Raw material availability
(ii) Market availability
(iii) Power and water availability
(iv) Access to trained human resources and specialization
(v) Basic facilities such as education and healthcare
(vi) Infrastructure such as roads
(vii) Safety and security
(viii) Environmental issues

After carefully considering the location, various facilities are to be established in that location with a suitable layout.

2.2 Layout criteria

Concerning the layout, the following types of problems may arise:

(i) On a location, various facilities are to be arranged from scratch. Therefore, a layout design is being sought.
(ii) A layout already exists; however, it needs to be changed after experiencing some issues or with an objective of improvement.
(iii) Out of a family of products, it is felt that a few products need a different kind of arrangement in order to increase efficiency.
(iv) Changes in the existing layout might be confined to very few facilities.

Factors affecting the layout are shown in Figure 2.10.

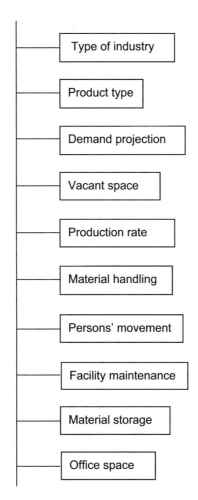

Figure 2.10 Factors affecting layout

2.2.1 *Type of industry*

The operational layout depends on the type of industry, such as:

 (i) Chemical
 (ii) Manufacturing
(iii) Agricultural
(iv) Service

In the case of the chemical industry, different processes are carried out one after another. Being a process industry including a continuous

37

process, a certain focus may also be on pipelines along with piping design in addition to facilities and storage tanks. Safety is also of prime concern. Similarly in petrochemical, fertilizer, and pharmaceutical companies, among others, the layout aspects should cover facilities, storage, safety, and related pipelines. Utilities such as water, steam, and air and their continuous flow at the desired parameters are to be ensured at the points of use. The desired parameters may include temperature, pressure, and humidity, among others.

In the manufacturing industry, various facilities may be installed in the sequence of operations to be carried out on the raw material/input item for standard products in substantial demands. However, when the variety of products is high with lower volumes, then the facilities may be arranged by department or their function. Normally the material/component is taken to various facilities on the shop floor. But suitable machines may also be taken to a place where very heavy material in large sizes is to be fabricated, such as in large ship building.

Seasonal procurement might be needed in the context of the agricultural industry, and therefore storage space might play an important role in addition to a suitable arrangement for concerned facilities in the layout. Utilization of cold storage related to fruits and vegetables may be kept in consideration while making suitable operational and investment decisions including facilities layout. In the production processes, a focus may be on material or input item movement. However, movement of persons may be considered specifically in service operations.

In services such as educational and hospital settings, the movement of persons can also be analyzed in addition to an appropriate arrangement of relevant facilities. Such facilities may include library materials, hospital equipment, and computer systems. Management of a variety of queues of persons should also be taken into consideration while designing the layout and subsequent creation of departments or facilities for a variety of services to be provided to people/customers.

2.2.2 Product type

What is the state the product is in at various stages of manufacturing, including the final stage? According to the different states, there are specific requirements for safe and smooth flow of material inside the plant. For example, the product may be in the form of a:

   (i) Solid
  (ii) Liquid
 (iii) Gas
 (iv) Gel
  (v) Paste

For instance, gas is also of different types and constituents, with specific characteristics. Liquid might be of kinds such as water and oil. The product might also be made of:

(i) Metal
(ii) Alloy
(iii) Wood
(iv) Glass
(v) Plastic
(vi) Composite material

These also vary in density, composition, and occupied space, which may be considered in storage and handling within the plant. Shape and size of the assembled part/final product also contribute towards storage and handling, such as:

(i) Ring/circular
(ii) Cylindrical
(iii) Spherical
(iv) Square
(v) Rectangular

Example 2.2

For instance, the L.P.G. cylinder has:

(i) A cylindrical body composed of upper and lower halves
(ii) Semi-ellipsoidal ends on the upper and lower halves
(iii) A valve protection ring on the top
(iv) A foot ring at the bottom

During storage, including temporary storage/work-in-process, it may be convenient to have two stacks. On the valve protection ring of one cylinder, the foot ring of another cylinder can rest. While handling on the shop floor, it is possible to have a grip on the valve protection ring, and the cylinder can be rolled on the foot ring along with a certain inclination.

2.2.3 Demand projection

In a case in which a company wishes to plan for its layout well in advance as per an increase in future demand, it may use a certain demand projection for the concerned product/activity. For this purpose, Table 2.3 may be useful.

The number of years for which demand is to be projected should be confined to only the duration/period in which a forecast is justified and reliable

Table 2.3 Projected demand

S. No.	1	2	3	4	5	6	7	8	9	10
Year										
Projected demand										

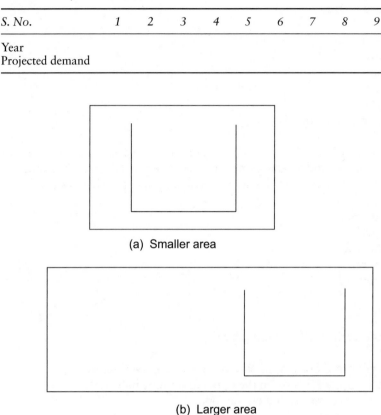

(a) Smaller area

(b) Larger area

Figure 2.11 Smaller/larger area

up to a reasonable extent. For example, a 'U' type of layout may be used for many products. Layout of the facilities is arranged in the location/area available. The organization may come across two situations, as shown in Figure 2.11, in which a layout is represented by 'U' in the available area that may be smaller or larger relatively.

Depending on the location, either a smaller or a larger area might be available for installing the facilities in a 'U' type of layout, for example. In the first situation, the area is just enough to be covered by the layout along with only essential space for additional activities, such as inbound and outbound logistics. In such a case, future expansion in terms of facilities/layout might be difficult. However, in the second case, enough space is available for expansion considering the potential demand increase. Having a smaller or larger area might depend on the following aspects:

  (i) Ownership of land for the last many years
 (ii) Price of the land in the case of a recent purchase
(iii) Rural/urban location
(iv) Availability constraint for the land
 (v) Negligible chance for a demand increase for a similar product

In order to accommodate future expansion in the context of a demand increase for a similar product (when a larger area is available to the organization), a variety of options are represented in Figure 2.12.

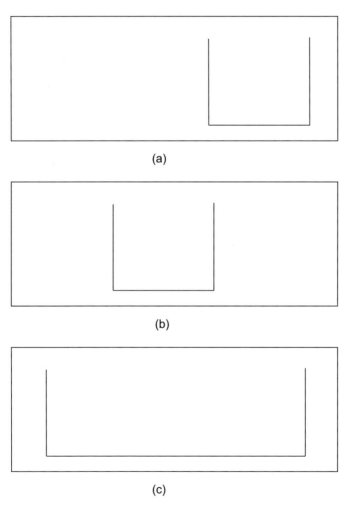

(a)

(b)

(c)

Figure 2.12 Options for arrangement of facilities

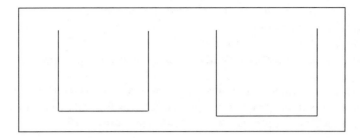

Figure 2.13 Adjacent similar layout

In option (a), the 'U' type of layout is available at one end of the larger area. For a future expansion corresponding to the demand, another more or less similar layout may be established adjacent to the existing one, as shown in Figure 2.13, with or without a partition. However, in option (b), the layout is at the centre of the area and the number of facilities may be increased at the outward side of the current layout in a future expansion. This might be more appropriate in the context of persons' movement and the balancing of workers and facilities in certain cases. Option (c) may not be desirable in most cases, as it covers the whole area presently and scope exists for an increase in the number of facilities at the inward side. Furthermore, when the need for expansion does not arise for a considerably longer period, the unnecessary movement of persons and materials happens throughout the area for a longer period.

2.2.4 Vacant space

Vacant space including that between the facilities may be needed for certain purposes, such as:

(i) Temporary storage for rejected components/products
(ii) Storage for work-in-process
(iii) Space for keeping the production lot for acceptance by customer/third-party/internal inspection at various stages

In the case in which provision for such space is insufficient, there might be a need to store the work-in-process inventories elsewhere within the premises slightly away from the production layout, leading to additional material handling. The requirement for such a space also depends on the production rate.

2.2.5 Production rate

If the production rate is higher, there is greater generation of volume. In practice, there is a difference in the production rate of facilities in the layout. For example, if the rate of production of a facility is more than that of a subsequent facility, then there is an accumulation of work-in-process inventory between these facilities if both are running simultaneously for a certain time. Analysis of production rate of various machines and the overall rate for the whole plant for the final product helps in planning for various objectives including the suitable layout with:

(i) Desirable number of similar facilities
(ii) Availability of space between the machines

2.2.6 Material movement

Movement of material happens in retail locations as well as in production layouts. Concerning the retail space, the following activities take place:

(i) The suppliers' representatives bring various items including FMCG for putting on the shelves of a big retail location. For the movement of trolleys carrying such items, sufficient space should be created in the overall layout of the retail location.
(ii) Consumers may put the items in trolleys after selecting them and take that towards the billing facility for payment and subsequent exit. A consideration needs to be made for enough space related to the movement of items including trolleys.

In the production house also, movement happens, such as for:

(i) Raw materials
(ii) Input items
(iii) Work-in-process
(iv) Finished products
(v) Variety of tools
(vi) Fuel

Accordingly, provision should be made for the smooth running of various production processes concerning the shop floor layout.

2.2.7 Persons' movement

Movement of people also plays an important role in some cases. For example, distance covered by a patient in a hospital is of concern. Careful decisions need to be made, such as:

(i) Where should the X-ray facility be installed?
(ii) Should the X-ray facility be nearer to the orthopaedics section?
(iii) What is a better place for the blood testing facility inside the hospital?

In the context of retail business, which sections should be placed together so that the consumer movement inside the premises would be largely preferred? As far as possible, the layout for keeping a variety of items should be such that the search for items becomes convenient for consumers. Additionally, enough space needs to be created for movement of consumers along with trolleys.

In a production house also, workers move for a variety of tasks, such as:

(i) Getting tools issued
(ii) Washing hands
(iii) Getting inspections done
(iv) Going between two machines related to the process

Accordingly, the provisions are created in the proposed layout so that the overall movement of workers is less and convenient also.

2.2.8 Facility maintenance

For the maintenance of facilities, the following tasks/issues may happen:

(i) A certain part of the machine is malfunctioning and needs to be replaced. Enough space should be available adjacent to such corners/sides of the machine for safe replacement of the part.
(ii) For ease in repair work, a subassembly of a facility needs to be taken out of the facility and would be taken elsewhere, such as a centralized maintenance room, where the problem in the subassembly would be identified for subsequent repair. In anticipation, a suitable space should be made available in the layout.

Depending on the case, care may be taken while designing the layout so that there is ease in the activities/provisions such as:

(i) Space for keeping the tools for maintenance work
(ii) Movement of equipment for repair/handling work
(iii) Movement of maintenance workers

2.2.9 Material storage

Sufficient storage space needs to be created for:

(i) Raw material
(ii) Finished products
(iii) Items used for variety of processes in the factory

Depending on the industrial operations, different raw materials may include steel, aluminium, wood, glass, and rubber. Raw material storage should be such that the space is utilized efficiently and also material is not spoiled. Issue of the material to the factory production should be convenient and not time-consuming. Finished products are also kept in certain designated spaces in the layout so that the packaging and dispatch to the customers are convenient and not time-consuming. Additionally, there are items needing storage for subsequent use concerning factory operations. These might include:

(i) Furnace oil
(ii) Welding electrode
(iii) Zinc wire

If problems arise in safe storage of such items, the production process may get affected, leading to higher costs.

Other than the factory operations including those required to run the facilities, spare parts storage is required for maintenance operations. These might include:

(i) Pressure relief valve
(ii) Oil seal
(iii) Solenoid valve
(iv) Gasket

On the basis of factors such as grouping of a variety of discussed materials/products, issue frequency, space to be occupied by various materials/parts, shelf life, and the possibility of spoilage, a suitable place may be designated for each item in the stores or warehouses.

Example 2.3

Welding electrodes are used substantially in the fabrication industry. In a factory, welding electrode packets were kept adjacent to the wall of the factory stores. During the rainy season, the wall became unusually damp (which did not happen before) because of exposure to the outside environment. This led to the packets catching moisture, affecting some of the welding electrodes. However, this was not noticed for a considerable period. At the end of the year, when the production cost was observed to be on the higher side, analysis was undertaken, along with the consideration of process cost accounting, among other measures.

After a detailed exercise, it became known that the consumption of welding electrodes was greater than the standard. Because of some moisture, it was relatively difficult to start the arc concerning the welding electrodes, and therefore breakage of electrodes happened along with greater consumption of this item during the fabrication process. Thus, the actual production cost was higher in comparison with the standard cost. The basic reason for this concerns the material storage.

2.2.10 Office space

Provision for office space inside an organization requires careful consideration. The factors affecting office space might include:

(i) Nature of work
(ii) Light and ventilation
(iii) Noise
(iv) Staff movement
(v) Level of thinking and planning involved

The nature of work may relate to production and service operations. Production operations concern industrial activities such as manufacturing, quality, and maintenance. Service operations may include hospital, education, and banking. As far as possible, enough light and ventilation should be arranged while designing and providing office space for a variety of personnel. Provision of natural light among other related aspects may be made if it is possible and convenient in the designed layout. Noise may affect the concentration of employees and their work. It also particularly affects hospital services. While arranging for the office space in general, certain care should be taken for an allowable noise level within the constraints with an objective of improving the productivity and satisfaction of all stakeholders.

While providing the office space, suitable consideration for staff movement, in order to avoid excessive fatigue, needs to be made that may include all relevant levels of employees, practitioners, and management, such as:

(i) Doctors, nurses, and compounders
(ii) Professors
(iii) Executives and managers

Different jobs require different levels of thinking and planning content. Accordingly, appropriate office space should be chosen in order to improve job quality, considering noise among other factors.

Example 2.4

In a transformer manufacturing company, it has been observed that a senior executive related to planning function has been given office space on the shop floor. Production activities such as winding, oven, and subassembly are happening on the same floor to which the mentioned office space is adjacent. An undesirable noise level is also observed in the office space. The function of this executive involves:

 (i) Inputs from marketing
 (ii) Prioritizing sales orders
(iii) Lead time consideration for various activities
(iv) Planning and scheduling for production
 (v) Replanning and rescheduling as per the need

As it is evident that a certain level of thinking and planning is involved, the job performance is getting affected because of noise and other disturbances in the office space. Frequent replanning and rescheduling are also observed, which could have been avoided up to a certain extent. In order to improve the performance, such an office space may be shifted to the first floor, that is, away from the production activities on the ground floor. From the functional productivity and satisfaction point of view, this may be helpful, as the first floor environment is relatively calm and quiet.

2.3 Material handling

Various departments are placed inside the layout so that the material handling efforts and the related cost can be minimized. For example, if there are three departments or sections as shown in Figure 2.14, then the objective may be to verify whether this arrangement is suitable from the material handling point of view.

An approach would be to estimate the flow of material in a specified period from one section to another. For instance, see Figure 2.15.

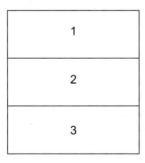

Figure 2.14 Three sections arrangement

1–2	30
1–3	180
2–3	50

Figure 2.15 Estimated material flow

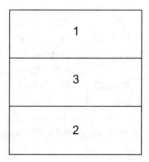

Figure 2.16 Modified arrangement for three sections

It can be observed that the flow volume from section 1 to section 3 is significantly higher than 1 to 2 and 2 to 3. Therefore, this arrangement may not be suitable from a material handling point of view, as sections 1 and 3 are relatively far away from each other. If sections 1 and 3 are closer to each other, it may be better. A modified arrangement is shown in Figure 2.16.

Either the arrangement is to be made from scratch in certain cases, or the existing setup may be modified if it is feasible, considering the investment and future savings because of this change. Additional aspects might be reverse flow also, as given here:

2–1
3–1
3–2

These should also be included in the analysis if such an estimated material flow exists for certain combinations of sections/departments.

Depending on the case, the following aspects may be considered in practice:

(i) Distance between any two sections
(ii) Multiplication of material flow and distance

(iii) Material handling cost
(iv) Whether one unit of item or several units of item are handled in one trip
 (v) Whether the number of trips between any two sections are relevant
(vi) Whether the material handling cost per unit item or such cost per trip is relevant
(vii) Role of material handling equipment

Example 2.5

In a large steel rolling mill established a few decades before, material handling is observed to be quite excessive because of the arrangement of sections/facilities in the layout. That is also affecting their competitiveness because new rolling mills have a more efficient layout and planned facilities setup with lower material handling efforts and cost.

During the process, steel remains in these two states:

 (i) Liquid state
(ii) Solid state

In the solid state, the product may be hot or room-temperature during the process. Some of the important facilities are as follows:

 (i) Furnace, such as electric arc furnace
 (ii) Continuous casting machine
(iii) Rolling mill
(iv) Straightening machine

With an objective of improving the layout along with a suitable arrangement of facilities, an analysis of material movement and handling is necessary. Table 2.4 may be useful for the purpose in general, for filling the relevant cells.

In order to collect the information, a suitable approach would involve identifying a few representative products for this purpose, since it is not

Table 2.4 Inter-facilities flow volume

From:	To: Facility #1	Facility#2	Facility #3	Facility #4 . . .
Facility #1				
Facility #2				
Facility #3				
.				
.				
.				

feasible to collect data for all products. For identifying the representative products of the company, the indicative factors are as follows:

(i) Customer/business value
(ii) Related revenue
(iii) Related profit
(iv) Strategic significance

After identification of a few representative products, an appropriate period should be determined in which material flow data are to be collected. Depending on considerable flow volume, this period can be a:

(i) Day
(ii) Week
(iii) Month
(iv) Quarter

In certain cases, year-wise data for material flow might also be available at the plant if such an effort has already been made.

After data collection, the facilities need to be identified that can be installed closer. However, a final recommendation would depend on aspects such as:

(i) Availability of space
(ii) Process sequence
(iii) Reinstallation cost
(iv) Savings related to material handling efforts/cost
(v) Payback period
(vi) Planning period

Wherever relevant, the material handling process and equipment may be taken into consideration.

There also might be a choice concerning:

(i) Reinstallation of identified facilities
(ii) Modified material handling process and equipment
(iii) Both (i) and (ii)

Example 2.6

Material flow analysis is also helpful for ease in handling the product/material or enhancing the flow speed. In case of the L.P.G. cylinder fabrication industry, a variety of tests are conducted for quality inspection purposes, including:

(i) Hydrostatic stretch test
(ii) Pre-pneumatic test
(iii) Final pneumatic test

For example, when production volume is not that great, one testing line related to the hydrostatic stretch test for L.P.G. cylinders might exist, as shown in Figure 2.17. On rollers, fabricated L.P.G. cylinders can enter from one side. The facility having an arrangement for filling water in the cylinder and then increasing the pressure inside the cylinder can appear on the top and side. It is to be observed whether there is any leakage from the cylinder. Then the cylinder can make an exit from the other side on rollers and finally be unloaded from such a facility.

When the production volume becomes greater, two testing facilities may be needed. For this purpose, an arrangement can be as shown in Figure 2.18.

However, two sets of workers are needed for handling the cylinders at entry and exit in the facility. For balancing the material flow and ease in handling with a lower requirement of workers, a preferred arrangement in most of the cases is as shown in Figure 2.19. One set of workers is suitable for the testing facilities at both entry and exit, that is, for keeping the cylinders on the rollers and unloading at the exit after the hydrostatic stretch test is carried out in both the testing facilities. A certain advantage can be gained by merging the material/product flow from the material handling point of view inside the layout of facilities.

With the rearrangement of facilities and testing centres in an existing organization, certain costs are incurred, which need to be carefully estimated. However, certain benefits are also potentially available and need to be projected carefully. Such costs and benefits should be analyzed

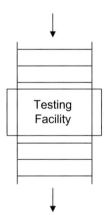

Figure 2.17 One testing line for the hydrostatic stretch test

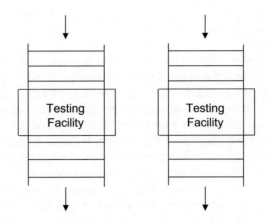

Figure 2.18 Two parallel testing lines for the hydrostatic stretch test

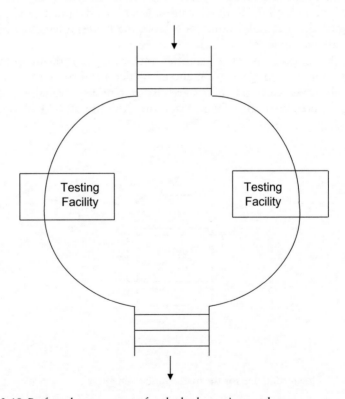

Figure 2.19 Preferred arrangement for the hydrostatic stretch test

along with consideration of multiple criteria. These criteria vary and may depend on:

(i) Type of industry
(ii) Budget allocation
(iii) Availability of finance
(iv) Availability of land
(v) Estimation of benefits
(vi) Visibility of benefits

2.4 Cost-benefit

Generally speaking, change in the layout for improvement in material handling, among other objectives, involves a certain expenditure; therefore, a rigorous cost-benefit analysis is also needed for final approval. Various factors related to costs or expenditure are shown in Figure 2.20.

In the context of machinery, two types of situations may emerge:

(i) In order to reduce the distance between the selected facilities, there is a need to reinstall. This requires a certain expenditure.
(ii) From a family of products, very few products or even one product are identified as having reasonably uniform demand with suitable volume. Currently this product is being processed along with others in a large layout. If a dedicated small space can be created where all the relevant

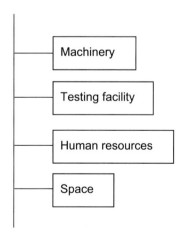

Figure 2.20 Cost-related factors

processes for this specific product are carried out at that location efficiently, it is expected to be of great help. However, entirely new and separate machinery might be needed. This requires substantial fixed cost/investment at this point in time and needs to be compared with the potential benefit for making a final decision.

In the context of testing facilities, the following situations may emerge:

(i) For ease in material handling, minor modifications are made in the selected testing facility. The place of such a testing facility may also change along with the reinstallation cost.
(ii) If a separate space is being created for the selected product where all the processes including inspection and testing are done, an entirely new testing facility is needed with costs such as purchase and installation.

Human resources may not contribute towards cost with an improvement in the existing layout. This is because human efforts and requirement for human resources are not supposed to increase with a modified layout. However, if a dedicated space is created for a certain specified product, as mentioned before, then obviously there may be a need for additional human resources related to the new facilities.

In a case in which space is needed for a layout change, the following situations may emerge:

(i) A sufficient area is already available with the organization.
(ii) Currently, such an area is not available and needs to be purchased if it is possible.

In the first situation regarding enough availability of area, analysis should be made whether it will impact any other activity in the case of its use in the layout. If it is so, such a lost opportunity cost should be estimated.

In the second situation, if the needed area is available adjacent to the existing premises and is available for purchase among other modes, such costs can be considered.

After arriving at the estimation of related costs, they need to be compared with the potential benefits. Different factors related to benefits are shown in Figure 2.21.

With the proposed layout, time taken by the input items inside the factory for processing and dispatch, that is, in-factory time, is expected to be reduced. Because of this proposed in-factory time reduction, the following may result:

(i) Due to this overall time reduction, the resources may be available for additional work, leading to an added value.
(ii) The possibility of more production volume in a day or suitable period may lead to a higher contribution.

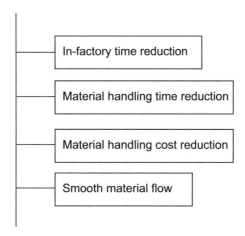

Figure 2.21 Benefit-related factors

(iii) In the case of items like food items, the remaining shelf life might become relatively longer if there is in-plant time reduction.

Material handling efforts and associated time get reduced with the modified layout and because of this, the material handling cost also decreases. Such costs are also reduced if more efficient equipment is deployed for handling the items/materials. After a suitable study, different equipment/modes of handling might be adopted for different items/materials. Without accumulation of idle work-in-process inventory, a smooth material flow may be considered as the potential benefit. These and associated benefits can be estimated/quantified in terms of money value. After the analysis of cost-benefit, an appropriate decision should be made regarding the layout and facilities.

SME's requirements with reference to cost-benefit comparison, among other aspects, would need further discussion. There might be situations in which cost or expenditure on location is borne by such an establishment or entrepreneur. Either a loan may not be so easily available or the entrepreneur doesn't want to take it. In a case in which a piece of land is readily available or it is their own, they may prefer to use it for the start of the business/ industry. In such a case or otherwise, there is limited choice in the context of location. This is because they may like to start from the place where they are based, instead of investing elsewhere.

The location characteristics are fixed and given, such as:

  (i) Either it is nearer to customers or farther away.
 (ii) Either it is nearer to raw material sources or farther away.
(iii) Either water is available continuously or not.
(iv) Either the power is available without any interruption or not.

(v) Either a good infrastructure is available from a logistical point of view or not.

(vi) Either there is availability of skilled workers or not.

At the given location, the available area may also have characteristics such as:

(i) Either small or large
(ii) Length is relatively much greater than width
(iii) Either square or rectangle, with not too much of difference in length and width of the available area

Given the location and available area, and in case of a disadvantage, additional efforts should be made to offset it by paying attention to the layout of facilities. The type of facilities and arrangement of those facilities can be suitably analyzed. For example, if the given area has much greater length than width, as shown in Figure 2.22, then the width may not be effectively utilized.

The facilities here need to be arranged length-wise. In such a scenario, material and person movement might be on the higher side, affecting the costs. Thus, general-purpose facilities, which may be less costly, can be installed if those are considered appropriate for the concerned business/product.

Exercises

1 What points should be taken into consideration first in order to locate an industrial or business organization?
2 What are the different objectives to establish various facilities in a location?

Figure 2.22 Representation of too much length relative to width

3 Explain the end consumer interaction in the context of following illustration:

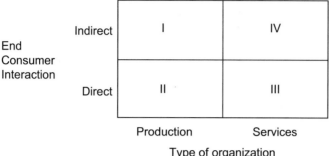

4 Discuss the consumer–company interaction in the context of the following illustration:

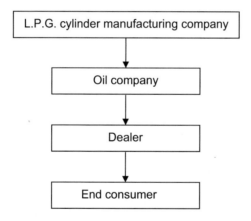

5 Explore the possibilities for location consideration in which a production organization has indirect interaction with the end consumer, such as:

(i) Near the end consumer
(ii) Away from the end consumer

6 Explore the possibilities for location consideration in which a production organization may like to have direct interaction with the end consumer, such as:

(i) Away from the end consumer
(ii) Near the end consumer

7 Explain the indirect relevance of major maintenance activities considering the following illustration:

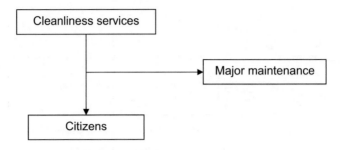

8 Discuss an interaction with the consumer company in the context of the following illustration:

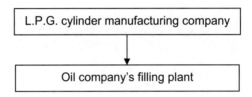

9 Describe the following aspects in the context of locational advantage:

   (i) Raw material availability
  (ii) Market availability
 (iii) Power and water availability
 (iv) Access to trained human resources and specialization
  (v) Basic facilities such as education and healthcare
 (vi) Infrastructure such as roads
(vii) Safety and security
(viii) Environmental issues

10 Explain the to-and-fro journey of used L.P.G. cylinders considering the following illustration:

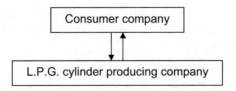

11 Discuss how the following types of problems may arise concerning the layout:

(i) In a location, various facilities are to be arranged from scratch. Therefore, a layout design is being sought.
(ii) A layout already exists; however, it needs to be changed after experiencing some issues or with an objective of improvement.
(iii) Out of a family of products, it is felt that a few products need a different kind of arrangement in order to increase efficiency.
(iv) Changes in the existing layout might be confined to very few facilities.

12 What are the factors affecting layout?

13 Elaborate how the operational layout depends on the type of industry, such as:

(i) Chemical
(ii) Manufacturing
(iii) Agricultural
(iv) Service

14 Consider the specific requirements for a safe and smooth flow of material inside the plant. With this scenario, explain when the product may be in the form of a:

(i) Solid
(ii) Liquid
(iii) Gas
(iv) Gel
(v) Paste

15 Consider the specific requirements for a safe and smooth flow of material inside the plant. With this scenario, explain when the product may be made of:

(i) Metal
(ii) Alloy
(iii) Wood
(iv) Glass
(v) Plastic
(vi) Composite material

16 Elaborate how the shape and size of the assembled part/final product also contribute towards storage and handling, such as:

(i) Ring/circular
(ii) Cylindrical
(iii) Spherical

(iv) Square

(v) Rectangular

17 Discuss the storage and handling when a product, for example, the L.P.G. cylinder, has:

(i) A cylindrical body composed of upper and lower halves

(ii) Semi-ellipsoidal ends on the upper and lower halves

(iii) A valve protection ring on the top

(iv) A foot ring at the bottom

18 Explain the demand projection in detail in the context of the following:

S. No.	1	2	3	4	5	6	7	8	9	10
Year										
Projected demand										

19 Discuss the role of vacant space, including that between facilities, for a certain purpose such as:

(i) Temporary storage for rejected components/products

(ii) Storage for work-in-process

(iii) Space for keeping the production lot for acceptance by customer/third-party/internal inspection at various stages

20 Comment on the following:

Analysis of production rate of various machines and the overall rate for the whole plant for the final product helps in planning for various objectives including a suitable layout with:

(i) A desirable number of similar facilities

(ii) Availability of space between the machines

21 Elaborate how in the production house, movement happens such as for:

(i) Raw materials

(ii) Input items

(iii) Work-in-process

(iv) Finished products

(v) A variety of tools

(vi) Fuel

22 Concerning the retail space, comment on the movement of items including trolleys and the need for space for activities such as the following:

(i) The suppliers' representatives bring various items including FMCG for putting on the shelves of a big retail location.

(ii) Consumers may put the items in trolleys after selecting them and take that towards the billing facility for payment and subsequent exit.

23 Regarding the movement of the people, discuss the approach related to the following:

(i) Where should the X-ray facility be installed?
(ii) Should the X-ray facility be nearer to the orthopaedics section?
(iii) What is a better place for the blood testing facility inside the hospital?

24 In a production house, describe workers' movement for variety of tasks such as:

(i) Getting tools issued
(ii) Washing hands
(iii) Getting inspections done
(iv) Moving between two machines related to the process

25 How can care be taken while designing the layout so that there is ease in activities/provision, such as:

(i) Space for keeping tools for maintenance work
(ii) Movement of equipment for repair/handling work
(iii) Movement of maintenance workers

26 Comment on the sufficient storage space to be created for:

(i) Raw material
(ii) Finished products
(iii) Items used for a variety of processes in the factory

27 Explain the storage requirements for items such as:

(i) Furnace oil
(ii) Welding electrodes
(iii) Zinc wire

28 Discuss the storage requirements for spare parts such as:

(i) Pressure relief valve
(ii) Oil seal
(iii) Solenoid valve
(iv) Gasket

29 Analyze the following situation:

Welding electrodes are used substantially in the fabrication industry. In a factory, welding electrode packets were kept adjacent to the wall of the factory stores. During the rainy season, the wall became unusually damp (which did not happen before) because of exposure to the outside environment. This led to the packets catching moisture, affecting some of the welding electrodes. However, this was not noticed for a considerable period. At the end of the year, when the production cost was observed to be on the higher side, analysis started happening along with the consideration of process cost accounting among other measures.

30 Describe the factors affecting office space such as:

    (i) Nature of work
    (ii) Light
    (iii) Ventilation
    (iv) Noise
    (v) Staff movement
    (vi) Level of thinking and planning involved

31 Analyze the following situation:

In a transformer manufacturing company, it has been observed that a senior executive related to planning function has been given office space on the shop floor. Production activities such as winding, oven, and sub-assembly are happening on the same floor to which the mentioned office space is adjacent. An undesirable noise level is also observed in the office space. The function of this executive involves:

    (i) Inputs from marketing
    (ii) Prioritizing sales orders
    (iii) Lead time consideration for various activities
    (iv) Planning and scheduling for production
    (v) Replanning and rescheduling as per the need

32 Assume that there are three departments or sections as follows:

1
2
3

There is a need to verify whether this arrangement is suitable from a material handling point of view. An approach would be to estimate the flow of material in a specified period from one section to another. It may be as follows:

1–2	35
1–3	190
2–3	55

Provide a modified arrangement for the three sections along with comments.

33 How might the following aspects be considered in practice?

   (i) Distance between any two sections
   (ii) Multiplication of material flow and distance
   (iii) Material handling cost
   (iv) Whether one unit of item or several units of item are handled in one trip
   (v) Whether the number of trips between any two sections are relevant
   (vi) Whether the material handling cost per unit item or such cost per trip is relevant
   (vii) Role of material handling equipment

34 In a large steel rolling mill established a few decades before, material handling is observed to be quite excessive because of the arrangement of sections/facilities in the layout. That is also affecting their competitiveness because new rolling mills have a more efficient layout and planned facilities setup with lower material handling efforts and cost.

   With an objective of improving the layout along with a suitable arrangement of facilities, explain how the following approach would be useful:

From:	To: Facility #1	Facility #2	Facility #3	Facility #4 . . .
Facility #1				
Facility #2				
Facility #3				
.				
.				
.				

35 To identify the representative products of a company, discuss the indicative factors such as:

   (i) Customer/business value
   (ii) Related revenue
   (iii) Related profit
   (iv) Strategic significance

36 Depending on considerable flow volume, how might the relevant period be identified as a:

   (i) Day
   (ii) Week

(iii) Month
(iv) Quarter

37 After data collection, the facilities need to be identified that can be installed closer. Elaborate how a final recommendation would depend on aspects such as:

(i) Availability of space
(ii) Process sequence
(iii) Reinstallation cost
(iv) Savings related to material handling efforts/cost
(v) Payback period
(vi) Planning period

38 Describe how a related choice concerning rearrangement of facilities might be:

(i) Reinstallation of identified facilities
(ii) Modified material handling process and equipment
(iii) Both (i) and (ii)

39 Material flow analysis is helpful for ease in handling the product/material or enhancing the flow speed. In case of the L.P.G. cylinder fabrication industry, a variety of tests are conducted for quality inspection purposes, including:

(i) Hydrostatic stretch test
(ii) Pre-pneumatic test
(iii) Final pneumatic test

For example, when production volume is not that much or considerable, one testing line related to the hydrostatic stretch test for L.P.G. cylinders might exist, as follows:

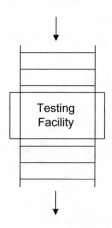

On rollers, fabricated L.P.G. cylinders can enter from one side. The facility having an arrangement for filling water in the cylinder and then increasing the pressure inside the cylinder can appear on the top and side. It is to be observed whether there is any leakage from the cylinder. Then the cylinder can make an exit from the other side on rollers and finally be unloaded from such a facility.

When production volume becomes higher, two testing facilities may be needed. For this purpose, discuss a variety of arrangements and also the preferred arrangement with the help of illustrations.

40 In the context of cost-benefit related to rearrangement of facilities and testing centres, explain criteria such as:

(i)   Type of industry
(ii) Budget allocation
(iii) Availability of finance
(iv) Availability of land
(v)   Estimation of benefits
(vi) Visibility of benefits

41 Concerning layout improvement, describe the cost-related factors, such as:

(i)   Machinery
(ii) Testing facilities
(iii) Human resources
(iv) Space

42 With the proposed layout, elaborate the benefit-related factors, such as:

(i)   In-factory time reduction
(ii) Material handling time reduction
(iii) Material handling cost reduction
(iv) Smooth material flow

43 Explain why the SME's requirements with reference to cost-benefit comparison among other aspects would need additional discussion.

44 Comment on the fixed and given location characteristics, such as:

(i)   Either it is nearer to customers or farther away.
(ii) Either it is nearer to raw material sources or farther away.
(iii) Either water is available continuously or not.
(iv) Either the power is available without any interruption or not.
(v)   Either a good infrastructure is available from a logistical point of view or not.
(vi) Either there is availability of skilled workers or not.

45 Comment on the available area characteristics in the given location, such as:

(i) Either small or large

(ii) Length is relatively much greater than width

(iii) Either square or rectangle with not too much of difference in length and width of the available area

46 Given the location and available area, and in case of a disadvantage, discuss what additional efforts should be made to offset it by paying attention to the layout of facilities.

3

PRODUCTIVITY CONSIDERATION

Productivity consideration deals with an effective utilization of resources, among other issues. Such resources may include facilities, manpower, and energy. Various industries are cautious of sources of energy as well as consumption. Some have captive power plants in addition to the energy purchase. However, the present focus is on the operational aspects and improvement in existing practices or processes so that energy consumption can be reduced. Additionally, the discussion can also be utilized for providing consultancy to SMEs. This is important because SMEs may not have captive power plants and depend solely on energy purchase. Thus, any suggested modification in processes or practices can help directly or indirectly in the reduction of energy consumption or the improvement in energy productivity.

After facilities are installed in a suitable location, the next important concern is how these work or are made operational with the use of relevant resources. This study needs to be done in the context of productivity, as productivity also affects profitability. Certain factors are usually taken into account in general, viz., an output level and an input criterion, while considering the productivity at an organizational level.

Generally speaking, productivity may be perceived as a ratio of output and input. A related nature of function may be concerned with the type of organization, such as manufacturing, educational, publishing, and project. Depending on the nature of function, different kinds of output (concerning a specified period like week, month, quarter, or year) may be perceived, such as teaching hours, number of complaints attended, number of inspections done, number of books published, production volume, projects completed, and number of repairs.

Current productivity related to any situation can be measured by considering relevant output and input, where the output is the numerator and the input is the denominator. In many cases, the current productivity measure can be used to compare the future scenario that might be improved or deteriorated. If there is an improvement, the productivity measure is enhanced and this is possible when:

(i) The numerator, that is, the output, has increased with a similar level of input.
(ii) The denominator, that is, the input level, has reduced with a similar level of output.
(iii) Both the numerator and the denominator, that is, the output and input, respectively, have varied in such a manner that the overall ratio has improved.

In a case in which both the output and input have varied, three possibilities emerge for productivity improvement. The first such possibility relates to the case in which output as well as input have increased, however the output increased more as compared to the input increase. The second instance concerns the scenario in which the output as well as input have decreased, however the output decreased less compared to the input decrease. The third possibility relates to the situation in which the output has increased with a decrease in input.

In the event of deterioration, the productivity measure decreases, and this happens when:

(i) Numerator, that is, the output level, has decreased with a similar level of input.
(ii) Denominator, that is, the input level, has increased with a similar level of output.
(iii) Both the numerator and denominator, that is, the output and input, respectively, have varied in such a manner that the overall ratio has been reduced.

In a case in which both the output and input have varied, three possibilities may emerge for productivity reduction. The first possibility relates to the situation in which the output as well as the input have decreased, however the output decreased more as compared to the input increase. The second possibility concerns the case in which the output as well as the input have increased, however the output increased less as compared to the input increase. The third possibility relates to the scenario in which the output level has decreased along with an increase in input. For a detailed analysis, the input resources should also be understood in the context of productivity for an appropriate measure.

Basically, performance of input resources are measured in a variety of specified outputs. Certain types of input resources are shown in Figure 3.1.

A machine or a group of machines can be considered an important resource. Its capacity and versatility may determine the possible range of output. The larger the number of machines, the higher the input level. With proper scheduling/loading of the machines, it may be possible to work with a

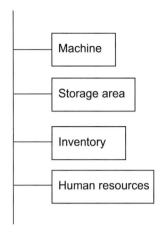

Figure 3.1 Input resources

smaller number of machines in order to achieve a similar production volume or output level. When several jobs with different requirements are queuing up before machines, then appropriate sequencing of jobs is also useful for an enhanced specified output level or desired goal.

Depending on the application, a storage area may refer to:

(i) Raw materials
(ii) Purchased components
(iii) Spare parts
(iv) Finished products
(v) Packaging materials

With proper planning, a larger volume of raw materials may be stored in a specified period. In a smaller storage area, a larger quantity of raw materials might be kept in a specified period. Among other aspects, this may also be possible by way of an improved storage rack design. The design and associated aspects might include the width and height of the storage racks as well as allocation of a particular raw material to a particular location or space in the rack. Similarly, in a storage area, more types and quantities of purchased components can be kept with certain efforts. Spare parts play a critical role in many situations in industrial or business activities. A facility may come to a complete breakdown or interruption, and a spare part might be needed. A wide variety of spare parts may need to be stored in different organizations. Depending on the nature of the business, spare parts may be used for activities such as maintenance of machines internally, maintenance of equipment/vehicles/machines outside, first-time assembly of equipment, or sales of spare parts.

Like raw materials, finished products are also stored for some time. This storage may be needed for want of demand or because of a waiting period concerning the arrival of trucks, among other possibilities. There is a possibility to use a smaller area for storing a greater variety of finished products and volumes in a specified period. Such possibilities can be explored related to the allocation of space for a particular product depending on weight/size and also frequency of issue/release. Similarly, packaging materials can be focused on for improvement in productivity pertaining to storage areas.

Inventory can be of various kinds, such as raw material or input items, work-in-process, and finished items. In cases in which the desired objective, such as a production plan, can be fulfilled with a lower inventory level, this may be preferred.

Human resources are deployed, and their productivity needs to be measured. In the case of human resources, it should be noted whether they are more or fewer for a desired task requirement. If they are more in number, idle time is considerable, which is nonproductive. On the other hand, the desired task objective either quantitatively or qualitatively gets affected with less manpower than what is required. Therefore, the optimization of human resources is necessary in the context of productivity.

3.1 Manpower productivity

There are different ways to measure the productivity of human resources or manpower productivity depending on the case under consideration. For example, production volume can be considered as an output, and the relevant input may be the number of workers. If the number of workers is similar and production volume is increased in a specified period, then the manpower productivity is presumed to increase. Alternatively, if a similar production volume is generated by a reduced number of workers in a specified period, then also the productivity can be considered to increase.

Example 3.1

In L.P.G. cylinder fabrication, mild steel sheets are sheared and then the circle cutting happens. Afterwards, many more processes are conducted. For convenience, consider only the three processes shown in Figure 3.2.

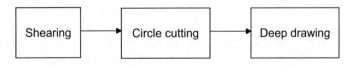

Figure 3.2 A part of the production process

The machines needed for these processes are as follows:

(i) Shearing machine
(ii) Circle-cutting machine
(iii) Hydraulic press

Traditionally, each machine may have two workers, that is, one skilled and one unskilled worker. However, it has been observed that the output of the hydraulic press, that is, the drawn cup shaped part or half, is a critical input to initiate subsequent processes. At least for this part of the production process, continuous feeding for the hydraulic press is important unless there is some obstruction ahead or space constraint for keeping the output of this press; this is also subject to the customer companies' orders. If this objective can be achieved subject to the aforementioned constraints, then simultaneous loading of the two upstream machines may not be necessary.

For satisfactory feeding of the hydraulic press, it is not necessary to run the following machines simultaneously:

(i) Shearing machine
(ii) Circle-cutting machine

It is feasible to offset these two processes in terms of time, and the same set of two workers associated with the shearing machine can be deployed to the circle-cutting machine also. Since both processes belong to sheet metal working, very little training/exposure would be enough for similar workers to handle both the processes at different time slots. With a certain focus on scheduling/loading the machines, it is possible to reduce the number of workers for this part of production process by two persons. A suitable production volume is generated for the main objective of continuous feeding of the hydraulic press in a specified period by a lower number of workers. Since, without affecting the overall production activity in terms of volume or output, the input level or number of workers has been reduced, manpower productivity can be considered to increase in a specified context. Furthermore, these now additionally available workers can be deployed elsewhere and such opportunities exist. If they are willing, job enrichment may also be available.

Such an exercise for manpower productivity can be extended throughout the organization. For the purpose of collecting the information and analyzing it, Table 3.1 may be useful.

Such a blank format as shown in Table 3.1 may be given to each section to fill up the existing details only or may be recorded by the consultancy team themselves. Afterwards, each section should be studied thoroughly regarding the production/inspection and other processes, and the proposed number of workers may be entered along with the reduction in manpower if any. A section-wise

71

Table 3.1 Human resources position

Section	Facility/ machine	Existing number of workers		Proposed number of workers		Reduction in manpower	
		Skilled	Unskilled	Skilled	Unskilled	Skilled	Unskilled

Table 3.2 Section-wise manpower position

Section	Existing number of workers		Proposed number of workers		Reduction in manpower	
	Skilled	Unskilled	Skilled	Unskilled	Skilled	Unskilled
Total						

summarized detail may also be provided, as shown in Table 3.2. The total of each column may be entered in the last row of this table as it is depicted.

Concerning all the sections in the organization, a total number of persons both skilled and unskilled would be available as follows:

(i) Existing
(ii) Proposed
(iii) Proposed reduction in manpower

Considering Table 3.1 with reference to an individual machine/facility, the following possibilities may emerge related to skilled as well as unskilled workers:

(i) Proposed number = Existing number
(ii) Proposed number > Existing number
(iii) Proposed number < Existing number

When the proposed number is similar to an existing number of workers, there seems to be no scope for improvement. The situation is already optimal or the number cannot be reduced within the constraints. In a certain case, it might be observed that the ideal strength should be higher than the existing scenario. In view of the consultancy team, if one person is added to the current strength for a group of machines, it will be helpful in sorting out the quality/maintenance issues better.

When the proposed number of persons is less than in the existing situation, then only the productivity improvement is found. In most of the cases of machines/facilities in the organization, the proposed number would be either equal to or less than the existing number if scope exists. For a certain facility, if the proposed number is greater than the existing number, this may be entered in Table 3.1 with an identification sign or within the bracket. However, in the summarized Table 3.2, net productivity improvement or reduction in the manpower appears section-wise. In the context of Table 3.2, the following possibilities may emerge:

(i) Overall productivity improvement or proposed reduction in number of persons appears for all the sections.
(ii) In a certain section, there is a proposed increase of persons overall. However, it is offset by the total reduction in other sections, and therefore a net total productivity improvement is concluded considering an overall organization-wide scenario.

Example 3.2

After the L.P.G. cylinder is completely fabricated, the following tests among others are conducted:

(i) Pre-pneumatic test
(ii) Final pneumatic test

In these pneumatic tests, compressed air is filled into the cylinder, and then the cylinder is dipped in a water tank. The test is done to check for any leakage of air in the form of bubbles in the water-filled tank. After the pre-pneumatic test, the following processes take place:

(i) Shot blasting
(ii) Metallizing
(iii) Primer coating
(iv) Final painting
(v) Valve fitting

Then the final pneumatic test is carried out for any potential leakage, including that from the valve.

Third-party inspection is necessary at certain stages before and after the pre-pneumatic test, such as after metallizing. For the pre-pneumatic as well as final pneumatic tests, one inspector and two workers are traditionally deployed from the organization side. Two different teams of one inspector and two workers each currently exist. After a study of certain aspects, there is a possibility of a similar team, that is, one team for both kinds of pneumatic tests, and thus manpower productivity improvement.

However, this may not be feasible for all organizations. The factor outside the organization is a third-party inspection process. In some cases, the relevant office is in close proximity and, therefore, visits for the purpose of third-party inspection can be more frequent or made available on demand. However, this is not so in some situations, that is, the relevant visits are infrequent and might not be precisely available on demand.

Depending on the case, it should be decided whether a similar team of one inspector and two workers should be deployed for both pre-pneumatic and final pneumatic tests without affecting the total relevant volume of production. Therefore, thorough scheduling within the organization helps a lot in this context, particularly taking into consideration the factors outside the organization such as the stage-wise third-party inspection. Concerning the third-party inspection, the considered aspects are as follows:

(i) How far the relevant office is
(ii) Degree of coordination efforts
(iii) Availability of persons in that office
(iv) Potential frequency of visits
(v) Potential time devoted per visit

Additionally, factors within the organization also lead to analysis, and these factors might be:

(i) Idle time of the team of one inspector and two workers
(ii) Testing facility setup time
(iii) Processing time
(iv) Space available for keeping the output of each test
(v) Availability of employees for creating different teams

Example 3.3

Consider the following situations:

(i) In the combination of skilled and unskilled workers, the number of unskilled workers is quite high.
(ii) In the combination of regular and contractual employees, the number of contractual employees is quite high.
(iii) In the opinion of the management, overtime is a significant issue within the organization.

(iv) The number of contractual employees or unskilled workers is fluctuating. In a certain region, the contractual labour strength depends on the agricultural season. In a particular season, they return to their villages to undertake the agricultural work and afterwards come back.

In the mentioned situations, the person-hours may be a suitable parameter to focus on for productivity improvement. Depending on the case, a focus may be on the overtime only or on the total time spent.

For example, in the heat treatment process, there are four unskilled workers and one skilled worker. Although the shift may be eight hours, the whole process may take more time because all the available batches of L.P.G. cylinders are to be heat-treated. Consider that this process takes ten hours for all the available batches cleared by the third-party inspection. Now the related person-hours are given by multiplication of number of persons and number of hours as follows:

$$5 \times 10 = 50$$

Assuming that the two unskilled workers have spent eight hours only, the related person-hours would be:

$$(2 \times 8) + (3 \times 10) = 16 + 30 = 46$$

Similarly, depending on the case, it is possible to keep the record at the level of:

(i) Facility
(ii) Section
(iii) Factory

And also, the period may be selected depending on the case, such as:

(i) Week
(ii) Month
(iii) Quarter
(iv) Year

For instance, section-wise data may be collected for the previous year and a cumulative figure is available for a total number of person-hours consumed in order to produce the annual output. A target may be decided to consume relatively fewer person-hours for a similar output next year, and it may be monitored periodically. In a case in which output varies, the output per unit person-hour might be the reference value for potential improvement by reducing the consumption of person-hours.

3.2 Human–machine interaction

In an organization, existing systems are available comprising machines/facilities and human beings and need to be observed closely. There are various facets of human–machine interaction, such as:

(i) In order to operate one machine or facility, how many workers are directly or indirectly engaged? Relevant engagement of persons happens for how much time?
(ii) Should one person operate one facility or more than one?
(iii) What is the suitable combination of number of persons (i.e., one or more) and number of machines (i.e., one or more)?

Example 3.4

In a pharmaceutical company, a portion of the production line is devoted to packaging the tablets, among other things. Persons' activities need to be synchronized with the packaging activities. For analyzing the scenario, some of the relevant aspects are shown in Figure 3.3, which pertains to the packaging of tablets.

Each strip consists of a few tablets. A few strips are then put in a packet. A few packets are put in a carton and then a few cartons are placed on a pallet. Additionally, the packaging speed can be observed, and it is possible to determine the outcome per unit time such as:

(i) Number of tablets
(ii) Number of strips
(iii) Number of packets
(iv) Number of cartons

If the number of persons is lower, palletizing may get delayed. On the other hand, if the number of persons is greater, idle time of the person can be

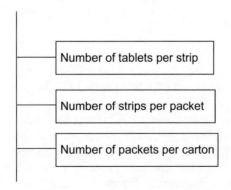

Figure 3.3 Aspects related to tablet packaging

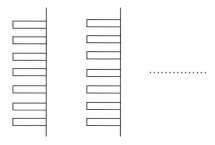

Figure 3.4 Representation of existing line alignment

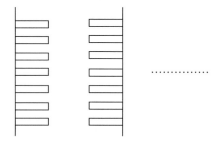

Figure 3.5 Representation of potential line alignment

observed. Accordingly, a suitable number of persons can be proposed. Additionally, the overall design/layout of the packaging lines may also be studied. For example, all the lines are aligned on one side, as shown in Figure 3.4. Traditionally, one person is deputed at the end of each line at the interface of cartons and pallets, among others. It is observed that the mentioned one person can handle the two lines if it is possible to change the alignment, as shown in Figure 3.5.

In this way, it is possible to reduce the number of persons to almost half for this specific activity. This may be possible after a thorough study of the interaction of human resources and the production/packaging line and also aspects such as:

(i) Whether the neighbouring lines are dedicated to similar tablets and for how much time
(ii) Whether the neighbouring lines are running simultaneously or there is a time offset
(iii) As per the past information, the stoppage pattern on account of frequency of setup, quality issues including breakage of tablet, and strip failure, among others

Example 3.5

In the case of a large retailer, the consumers pick the retail items. After picking, these consumers bring the items to the billing facility with the bar code reader. A certain space is often convenient to keep the items at the inlet side, as shown in Figure 3.6.

At the inlet side, consumers often remove the items one after another from the trolley. At each billing facility, two employees are often available. One person takes each item to the bar code reader and, as it is entered into the system, the items are transferred to the adjacent space for keeping the items in a suitable bag by another person. After bill generation and payment, consumers can take the bags filled with their purchased items at the outlet side.

It has been observed that many customers have to wait for a longer time at inlet sides of the billing facilities. In order to reduce the waiting time and congestion, an easily visible option is to increase the number of billing facilities. However, further close observation reveals the following:

(i) As the total area is similar, extra space may be made available by contraction in the existing space for keeping the items on shelves. This might not be desirable.
(ii) Extra space for an increase in the number of billing facilities might be made available from some space for movement of consumers and also trolleys, among other things. This also might not be a desirable option.

After a detailed study of the consumers at the inlet side and operations of the billing facility including employees, it has been observed that the length of the space at the inlet side for keeping the items is unnecessarily too much. If this length for space at the inlet side is reduced, as shown in Figure 3.7, enough space is released considering all the billing facilities that exist now.

Thus, the released area can be utilized for increasing the number of billing facilities. This is implemented without affecting the existing space for:

(i) Keeping the items on shelves
(ii) Movement of the consumers

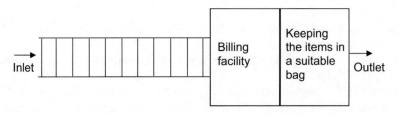

Figure 3.6 Billing facility at a large retailer

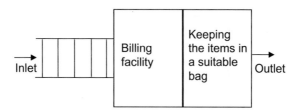

Figure 3.7 Representation of reduced length of space at inlet side

(iii) Trolley handling
(iv) Replenishing the items on shelves by the representatives of various suppliers

Example 3.6

A container and freight forwarding agency receives the following types of goods for forwarding:

 (i) Imported goods containers loaded on the trucks
(ii) Export goods containers loaded on the trucks

In the context of imports, ships arrive with the containers. These containers are reloaded on trucks after unloading and completion of formalities. From the dock, trucks carrying containers reach the agency premises. After the arrival and certain paperwork, goods in the containers are ready for forwarding to the customer organizations.

In the context of exports, goods are stuffed into the containers, and trucks carrying containers leave for the dock for onward shipping. In this way, stuffing and de-stuffing the containers would become frequent activities with deployment of workers. Different parameters can be evolved, such as the time spent by the truck inside the premises and also the time spent by the workforce in activities like stuffing and de-stuffing the containers.

Because the organization may deal with several items, and it is not possible to study all of them, one or more strategic items should be identified. Examples are the items that are frequently handled or the items that contribute to significant business value. Presently, the company handles a wide variety of items, such as:

  (i) Agricultural items
 (ii) Pharmaceutical products
(iii) Engineering items

Among agricultural items also, a variation exists that ranges from food grains to cotton; that is, the items differ in weight and volume as well as handling/packing requirements. Pharmaceutical products include medicines such as tablets and also equipment. Engineering items also differ in size and weight. With reference to the business value, a broad category of items may be found and then the focus may be on one or more items from one or more categories depending on the need and time available for the study.

For a detailed study, Table 3.3 may be useful to collect the information concerning select items.

After the description of an activity, time consumed is finally recorded, along with the resources used. Time consumed is the difference between the finish time and the start time of an activity. Resources used may include human resources and equipment such as a forklift truck and crane. For instance, activity may begin at the truck entry from the gate. Before opening the gate, a security person checks the papers and then allows the truck to enter.

On one side of the gate, there is a security office and on another side of the gate, there is space for an executive to do detailed paperwork and an entry into the system. After entry into the premises from the gate, the truck still stops for detailed paperwork and entries into the system. Then it is released for subsequent activities in another area, such as unloading or de-stuffing of the container carrying imported goods.

After system entries, resources such as the workforce, forklift truck, and crane are arranged as per the precise need. It has been observed many times that:

(i) A truck has reached the right place for subsequent activities; however, one or more desired resources are not available.
(ii) Resources are readily available; however, the truck could not reach the right place within the premises.

In order to reduce the time spent by trucks within the premises, every activity should be critically analyzed with reference to the time consumed and the way it is done. This is an essential step to suggest any potential improvement. As mentioned before, this process may start from the entry into the gate. The representation of closed and open doors is shown in Figure 3.8.

The door opens on both sides manually by the security person after preliminary checking of the papers concerning the truck. In the context of frequent entry and exit, if the door arrangement is changed, it may save

Table 3.3 Activity details

Activity description	Start time	Finish time	Time consumed	Resources used

Figure 3.8 Existing representation of door

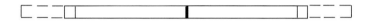

Figure 3.9 Desirable representation of door

considerable total time throughout the day. A desirable representation for the door is shown in Figure 3.9.

The door may open and close in a similar plane with the help of a little automation and change in design.

Additionally, certain coordination related to truck movement and organizing the resources helps in avoiding or minimizing the occurrence of the following situations:

(i) A truck is available at the right place in the premises; however, one or more resources are not available.
(ii) Resources are available at the right place in the premises; however, the presence of a truck could not be ensured for some time.

Such efforts help in minimizing the time spent by trucks inside the premises as well as nonproductive time related to the resources including the workforce.

3.3 Energy criteria

The energy criteria may relate to its effective utilization in all forms. Energy auditing is usually a significant step in an organization to know the precise energy consumption at various stages. Initially, a few areas can be identified where maximum consumption or improvement opportunities exist. Those few areas can be focused on with an objective of suggesting improvement.

However, in general, it is also possible to measure the actual energy consumption related to a running facility with the help of available devices for a certain period and compare that with the theoretical consumption. In the case of a considerable gap between theoretical and actual consumption, the reasons should be investigated. Recommendations can then be made with

Table 3.4 Theoretical and actual energy consumption

Facility	Theoretical consumption	Actual consumption	Considerable gap, if any	Potential reasons

an aim to eliminate the significant reason. For collecting the information, Table 3.4 may be useful.

Depending on the application, some of the possible reasons for the energy losses can be:

(i) Heat loss
(ii) Insulation
(iii) Door closure
(iv) Calibration
(v) Illumination
(vi) Friction
(vii) Leakages

For example, in the case of an oil-fired furnace, heat loss might be observed at the interface of:

(i) Door and inlet side
(ii) Door and outlet side
(iii) Burner and furnace wall

Insulation helps in losses, and also door closure practices should be observed. Calibration of various equipment for measurement helps indirectly in prevention of losses. Generally speaking, proper illumination including natural light may contribute towards lowering electricity consumption. Friction in the machine parts may be avoided to lower the power consumption in order to run the machine(s). As far as possible, leakages such as those of air, water, and steam should be plugged in order to gain overall advantages.

Example 3.7

Compressed air and its flow have several utilities in an industrial organization, such as pneumatic testing, internal cleaning, as well as drying. As shown in Figure 3.10, the output of an air compressor, among other applications, goes to the shot blasting machine.

The shot blasting machine uses shots that are thrown with high velocity on a surface or object along with compressed air through nozzles. The output of the compressor is accumulated in a compressed air storage tank

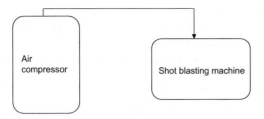

Figure 3.10 Compressed air to shot blasting machine

and certain pressure is maintained in that tank. From the storage tank, compressed air is taken to different application points through pipelines. It also goes to the shot blasting machine, whose application is to clean the surface or object for further processes, among other objectives.

It has been observed that there is relatively more rework concerning the shot blasting machine. Among other reasons, a drop in air pressure leads to malfunctioning of the machine and therefore the surface is not cleaned properly in one go. Due to this, repetition or rework happens for a certain number of products, and the energy consumption per unit product becomes higher related to this process.

In the context of energy criteria, the productivity may be said to increase if:

(i) Relevant volume of production is greater with similar power consumption.
(ii) Power consumption reduces for similar relevant production volume.
(iii) Reduced power consumption per unit production is observed.

Because of an undesirable pressure drop at the shot blasting machine, another facility, that is, the air compressor, also has to work more, leading to further energy consumption. It has been noticed that the distance between these two facilities is longer relatively. Because of this, the lengths of pipeline including bends and directional changes are greater, contributing to losses. A representation of a longer distance is also shown in Figure 3.11.

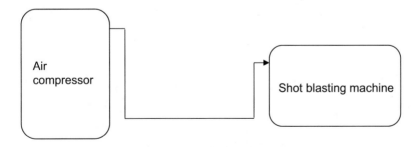

Figure 3.11 Representation of longer distance with bends

Because of the possibility to install an air compressor along with the storage tank, adjacent to the shot blasting machine, it needs to be implemented. This is because of a decrease in pipeline length along with elimination of bends and directional changes. However, the following should be analyzed:

 (i) Whether favourable space is available without affecting other operations
(ii) Whether the cost of reinstallation is justified

Presently, enough adjacent space is available and the reinstallation cost is justified with reference to:

 (i) The potential benefit
(ii) A suitable payback period

Therefore, this is finally implemented, ensuring a reduced energy consumption per unit production, thus leading to a productivity improvement with reference to energy criteria. A representation of a reduced pipeline length is also shown in Figure 3.12.

When the energy consumption is lower for a particular task, certain improvement is said to happen in view of energy criterion. Some related areas are shown in Figure 3.13.

Energy-efficient ways of material handling within the organization have to be found. In addition to the type of material handling equipment being used, this also relates to the quantity being handled in one trip. Analysis may also happen whether the reverse trip is empty or productive, that is, whether a certain material is being handled in a reverse trip also. In order to make more productive use of equipment, frequency with which material is being handled in a specified period currently has a role to play.

Transportation outside the organization might be in terms of inbound and outbound logistics. The following questions may be asked:

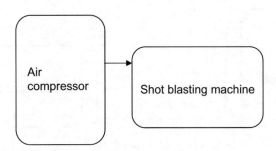

Figure 3.12 Representation of adjacent facilities

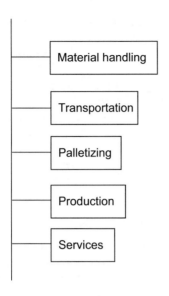

Figure 3.13 Some areas in view of energy criteria

(i) What quantity of input items is being transported? And with what frequency?
(ii) Which transportation medium is being used for input items? And with how much fuel consumption?
(iii) What quantity of output items is being transported? And with what frequency?
(iv) Which transportation medium is being used for output items? And with how much fuel consumption?

After a detailed study, changes might be possible in terms of:

(i) Suitable transportation medium
(ii) Size/capacity of transportation medium
(iii) Scope for productive return trip
(iv) Frequency of transport

If fuel consumption can be reduced, it is a significant step towards overall energy productivity.

In the context of palletizing, the material of pallets can be studied. Additionally, the design and weight of the pallets are of significance. Possibilities are to be explored to make it light in weight either by change in design or substitution of material or both. A lightweight pallet may help in ease in handling as well as indirectly in energy savings.

85

All the production activities including manufacturing and quality testing can be studied from the point of view of energy criteria. A feasibility study related to the equipment and process with lower energy consumption should be conducted.

Services are of a wide variety. For instance, food preparation in catering services within the organization might be paid some attention. If the food is prepared well in advance, there may be a need to store it in a warm or cold environment for a relatively longer period, thus leading to a less energy-efficient practice. Synchronization or coordination related to food preparation and consumption might contribute towards more energy-efficient catering services.

3.4 Benchmarking

Benchmarking relates to the comparison of an area or activity under consideration with that perceived to be the best. Global benchmarking might take place with reference to the best globally. However, while benchmarking, the following aspects should be considered before a relevant comparison:

(i) What is the current state of affairs?
(ii) Are all the clearly visible drawbacks/shortcomings addressed properly?

Additionally, while benchmarking, details should be considered, such as:

   (i) Country
  (ii) State
 (iii) Environment/atmosphere/weather
 (iv) Political scenario
  (v) Social aspects
 (vi) Culture
(vii) Working habits
(viii) Income levels
 (ix) Facilities standards
  (x) Infrastructure

However, a general procedure for benchmarking is represented in Figure 3.14. There are different types of areas, such as:

 (i) Procurement
(ii) Logistics
(iii) Production
(iv) Marketing
 (v) Finance
(vi) Automation

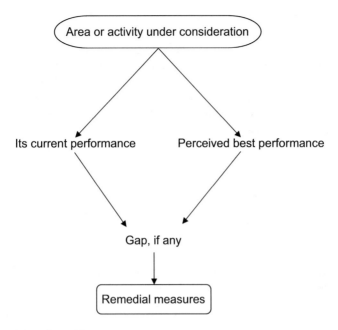

Figure 3.14 Benchmarking process

In each area, there are different activities, and a variety of performance measures can be developed for each activity. Among others, those might pertain to:

  (i) Human resources
 (ii) Production
(iii) Machine
(iv) Quality
 (v) Maintenance
(vi) Energy
(vii) Environment

Current performance is evaluated with the use of certain measures, and it is compared with the perceived best performance. If there is any gap in these two, that is, if current performance is lower than the best, remedial steps should be taken. Remedy may be in the form of:

  (i) Finding the root cause of the problem
 (ii) Rectification steps
(iii) Implementing best practices

However, sufficient care should be taken while adopting the practices of another organization that is perceived to be the best. This is because each company may have a distinct operational framework and also geographical area, among other aspects.

For example, one performance measure can be inventory turnover ratio. Ideally, a high ratio is preferred. However, the prime objectives are customer satisfaction and fulfilling the order on time, and those should not suffer on account of maintaining the best ratio. In a case in which the outsourcing level is very high, a similar inventory ratio may not be desirable, that is, belonging to another company in which the outsourcing level is not comparable. A final decision to keep an appropriate inventory turnover ratio, in addition to outsourcing level, may also depend on:

(i) Supplier relationship
(ii) Understanding of supplier operations and control
(iii) Level of cooperation
(iv) Level of coordination and communication

An SME's perspective needs further discussion concerned with benchmarking, among other aspects. While benchmarking and assessing the situation, the criteria as shown in Figure 3.15 should also be included.

When facility or technology employed is considered, it should be seen whether it can produce a certain level of quality. Productivity is also linked to the rejection percentage while using a certain facility. With the use of an existing facility, the information should be included related to the corresponding normal percentage of rejection. In the context of downtime or

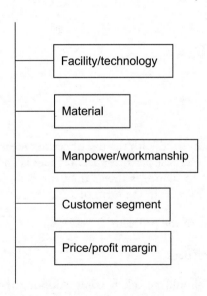

Figure 3.15 Criteria from an SME's perspective

uptime related to maintenance aspects, it should be noted whether a certain benchmark is relevant with the existing facility.

The greater the rework on the facility, the less is the productivity. Material or combination of materials used for the manufacture of product also affects the level of rework. Depending on the source of material and composition, the level of rework varies. It also might be possible that the SMEs are advised to purchase the material from a particular source for a certain portion of their requirements.

The following should be observed in the context of SMEs:

(i) What kind of manpower in terms of qualification, skill, and experience is available?
(ii) What kind of training arrangement for the manpower is available?
(iii) What is the employee attrition rate?

With the existing scenario of human resources, it should be determined whether the desired workmanship is possible.

As quality is a relative term, the customer segment that the SMEs presently are serving might be satisfied. Price of their product is also an important criterion. Depending on the profit margin available, further investment might be concerned with:

(i) Technology
(ii) Innovation
(iii) Workforce
(iv) Marketing

Exercises

1 With reference to productivity, discuss what you understand by the following factors:

  (i) Output level
  (ii) Input criterion

2 Depending on the nature of function, explain different kinds of output (concerning a specified period), such as:

  (i) Teaching hours
  (ii) Number of complaints attended
  (iii) Number of inspections done
  (iv) Number of books published
  (v) Production volume
  (vi) Projects completed
  (vii) Number of repairs

3 Comment on the current productivity measures.
4 Discuss what you understand by input resources, such as:

(i) Machine
(ii) Storage area
(iii) Inventory
(iv) Human resources

5 Explain the following situations when:

(i) Output has changed
(ii) Input has varied
(iii) Both output and input have varied

6 Explain the storage area in the context of productivity for:

(i) Raw materials
(ii) Purchased components
(iii) Spare parts
(iv) Finished products
(v) Packaging materials

7 What are different ways to measure the productivity of human resources or manpower productivity depending on the case under consideration?
8 Discuss the productivity in the context of machine or facility.
9 In L.P.G. cylinder fabrication, mild steel sheets are sheared and then the circle cutting happens. Afterwards, many further processes are conducted. For convenience, consider only the three processes as follows:

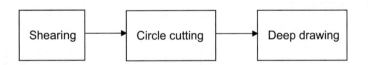

The machines needed for these processes are as follows:

(i) Shearing machine
(ii) Circle-cutting machine
(iii) Hydraulic press

Traditionally each machine may have two workers, that is, one skilled and one unskilled worker. However, it has been observed that the output of the hydraulic press, that is, the drawn cup shaped part or half, is a critical input to initiate subsequent processes. At least for this part of the production process, continuous feeding for the hydraulic press is important unless there is some obstruction ahead or space constraint for keeping the output of this press; this is also subject to the customer companies' orders. If this objective can be achieved subject to the aforementioned constraints, then simultaneous loading of the two upstream machines may not be necessary.

Comment on the feasibility to offset these two upstream processes in terms of time and also the possibility when the same set of two workers associated with the shearing machine can be deployed for the circle-cutting machine.

10 Describe how the following table is useful for further analysis related to manpower productivity:

Section	Facility/ machine	Existing number of workers		Proposed number of workers		Reduction in manpower	
		Skilled	Unskilled	Skilled	Unskilled	Skilled	Unskilled

11 Explain the following possibilities that may emerge related to the skilled as well as unskilled workers:

(i) Proposed number = Existing number
(ii) Proposed number > Existing number
(iii) Proposed number < Existing number

12 After the L.P.G. cylinder is completely fabricated, the following tests among others are conducted:

(i) Pre-pneumatic test
(ii) Final pneumatic test

In these pneumatic tests, compressed air is filled in the cylinder and then the cylinder is dipped in a water tank. The test is done to check for any leakage of air in the form of bubbles in the water-filled tank. After the pre-pneumatic test, the following processes take place:

(i) Shot blasting
(ii) Metallizing
(iii) Primer coating
(iv) Final painting
(v) Valve fitting

Then the final pneumatic test is carried out for any potential leakage including that from the valve.

Third-party inspection is necessary at certain stages before and after the pre-pneumatic test such as after metallizing. For the pre-pneumatic as well as final pneumatic tests, one inspector and two workers are traditionally deployed from the organization side. Two different teams of one inspector and two workers each currently exist. After a study of certain aspects, explore the possibility of a similar team, that is, one team for both kinds of pneumatic tests, and thus a manpower productivity improvement.

13 Comment on the following situations for a suitable parameter to focus on for productivity improvement:

(i) In the combination of skilled and unskilled workers, the number of unskilled workers is quite high.

(ii) In the combination of regular and contractual employees, the number of contractual employees is quite high.

(iii) In the opinion of the management, overtime is a significant issue within the organization.

(iv) The number of contractual employees or unskilled workers is fluctuating. In a certain region, the contractual labour strength depends on the agricultural season. In a particular season, they return to their villages to undertake agricultural work and afterwards come back.

14 Explain the various facets of human–machine interaction, such as:

(i) In order to operate one machine or facility, how many workers are directly or indirectly engaged? Relevant engagement of persons happens for how much time?

(ii) Should one person or more than one operate one facility?

(iii) What is the suitable combination of number of persons (i.e., one or more) and number of machines (i.e., one or more)?

15 Discuss how, in a pharmaceutical company, the following aspects are relevant:

(i) Number of tablets per strip

(ii) Number of strips per packet

(iii) Number of packets per carton

16 Elaborate why in a pharmaceutical company, there is a need to determine the outcome per unit time, such as:

(i) Number of tablets

(ii) Number of strips

(iii) Number of packets

(iv) Number of cartons

17 If there are fewer persons in packaging lines for medicines, palletizing may get delayed. On the other hand, there are more persons, idle time of the person can be observed. Accordingly, a suitable number of persons can be proposed. Additionally, the overall design/layout of the packaging lines may be studied. For example, all the lines are aligned on one side as follows:

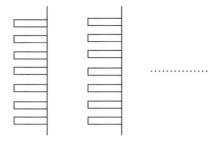

Traditionally, one person is deputed at the end of each line at the interface of carton and pallet, among others. It is observed that the mentioned one person can handle two lines if it is possible to change the alignment. Describe the potential or modified line alignment with the help of an illustration.

18 Consider the billing facility at a large retailer. At the inlet side, consumers often remove the items one after another from the trolley. At each billing facility, two employees are often available. One person takes each item to the bar code reader and, as it is entered into the system, the items are transferred to the adjacent space for keeping the items in a suitable bag by another person. After bill generation and payment, consumers can take the bags filled with their purchased items at the outlet side.

It has been observed that many customers have to wait for a longer time at inlet sides of the billing facilities. Explore various options along with:

(i) Advantage
(ii) Disadvantage
(iii) Implementation

19 A container and freight forwarding agency receives the following type of goods for forwarding:

(i) Imported goods containers loaded on trucks
(ii) Export goods containers loaded on trucks

In the context of imports, ships arrive with the containers. These containers are reloaded on trucks after unloading and completion of formalities. From the dock, trucks carrying containers reach the agency premises. After the arrival and certain paperwork, goods in the containers are ready for forwarding to the customer organizations.

In the context of exports, goods are stuffed into the containers, and trucks carrying containers leave for the dock for onward shipping. In this way, stuffing and de-stuffing the containers would become frequent activities with deployment of workers. Different parameters can be evolved, such as the time spent by trucks inside the premises and also the time spent by the workforce in activities like stuffing and de-stuffing the containers.

Elaborate how the following is useful for a detailed study:

Activity description	Start time	Finish time	Time consumed	Resources used

20 Explain how, in the context of energy criteria, the following is helpful:

Facility	Theoretical consumption	Actual consumption	Considerable gap, if any	Potential reasons

21 Discuss some of the possible reasons for energy losses, such as:

 (i) Heat loss
 (ii) Insulation
 (iii) Door closure
 (iv) Calibration
 (v) Illumination
 (vi) Friction
 (vii) Leakages

22 Describe the following areas in view of energy criteria:

 (i) Material handling
 (ii) Palletizing
 (iii) Transportation
 (iv) Production
 (v) Services

23 Provide a detailed comment on the following.
 In the context of energy criteria, productivity may be said to increase if

 (i) Relevant volume of production is more with similar power consumption
 (ii) Power consumption is reduced for similar relevant production volume
 (iii) Reduced power consumption per unit production is observed

24 While benchmarking, explain how the following aspects should be considered before a relevant comparison:

 (i) What is the current state of affairs?
 (ii) Are all the clearly visible drawbacks/shortcomings addressed properly?

25 Additionally, while benchmarking, elaborate why details should be considered such as:

  (i) Country
  (ii) State
  (iii) Environment/atmosphere/weather
  (iv) Political scenario
  (v) Social aspects
  (vi) Culture
  (vii) Working habits
  (viii) Income levels
  (ix) Facilities standards
  (x) Infrastructure

26 Current performance is evaluated with the use of certain measures, and it is compared with the perceived best performance. If there is any gap in these two, that is, if current performance is less than the best, remedial steps should be taken. Describe how a remedy may be in the form of:

  (i) Finding the root cause of the problem
  (ii) Rectification steps
  (iii) Implementing best practices

27 One performance measure can be inventory turnover ratio. Ideally, a high ratio is preferred. However, the prime objectives are customer satisfaction and fulfilling the order on time, and those should not suffer on account of maintaining the best ratio. In a case in which the outsourcing level is very high, a similar inventory ratio may not be desirable, that is, belonging to another company where the outsourcing level is not comparable. Discuss in detail how a final decision to keep an appropriate inventory turnover ratio, in addition to the outsourcing level, may also depend on:

  (i) Supplier relationship
  (ii) Understanding of supplier operations and control
  (iii) Level of cooperation
  (iv) Level of coordination and communication

28 An SME's perspective needs further discussion concerned with benchmarking, among other aspects. While benchmarking and assessing the situation, comment on the inclusion of criteria such as:

  (i) Facility
  (ii) Technology
  (iii) Material
  (iv) Manpower
  (v) Workmanship
  (vi) Customer segment

(vii) Price
(viii) Profit margin

29 Explain how, depending on the profit margin available, further investment might be concerned with:

(i) Technology
(ii) Innovation
(iii) Workforce
(iv) Marketing

30 Elaborate on the following in the context of SMEs, among others:

(i) What kind of manpower in terms of qualification, skill, and experience is available?
(ii) What kind of training arrangement for the manpower is available?
(iii) What is the employee attrition rate?

4

LEAD TIME OBJECTIVE

A major factor for competitiveness in the manufacturing as well as services industry is lead time. This chapter focuses on an introduction of this parameter in addition to other significant details. As a practitioner approach is followed in the context of industrial consultancy, appropriate case studies and examples are provided in order to understand the concept and practices as well as improvements in existing practices.

Lead time is the time span between the point of time when actual services are performed and that when an order was placed for services. As shown in Figure 4.1, lead time can be associated with service operations and production operations.

However, there may also be a combination of service and production operations in some cases.

4.1 Lead time's role

Lead time has a role to play in multiple situations, some of which are shown in Figure 4.2.

In case of hotel/catering services, a customer orders for lunch for example at 1:00 PM after reaching the concerned hotel. However, he or she is able to take the lunch at 2:00 PM only because the staff took one hour to prepare and bring it to the table. In this case, the lead time is one hour.

The lead time might have implications as follows:

 (i) The customer is not willing to wait for such a time span and therefore may not visit again.
(ii) If it is possible, the customer may cancel the order.

In the first scenario, potential sales are lost, whereas in the second scenario present as well as potential sales might be lost.

However, if a group of persons visits the place and has a plan to discuss some important issues over lunch for one to two hours, this particular lead time is not problematic for them. Therefore, a longer lead time may not be

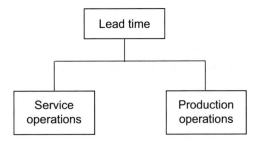

Figure 4.1 Operational lead time

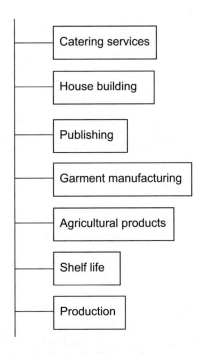

Figure 4.2 Some situations having a lead time role

bad all the time. A suitable lead time depends on the customers and their desired objective in addition to the producer resources and constraints.

In the case of building a house, quite often a deadline may not be met. Among other reasons, this is because one or other components of the lead time takes longer than expected. Relevant components of the lead time may include:

(i) Selection of the location
(ii) Procurement of the land
(iii) Procurement for related building materials at various stages

(iv) Construction of the house
(v) Finishing and electricity fitting
(vi) Final handing over/taking over

In the publishing industry, for example, if a book is not published within a suitable time, then there is a possibility of losing its positive effects up to a certain extent. Similarly, in the case of a product like a garment, these should be available at the right time in the market. Accordingly, all the concerned agencies should adhere to the planned lead time.

Agricultural items like food grain may be available in a certain season at the right price in abundance. Accordingly, the procurement plan should be made considering the relevant lead time. Shelf life also has a role in food items, including freshness. Generally speaking, shelf life has a significant role in planning the lead time pertaining to products including milk, curd, fruits, vegetables, and pharmaceuticals.

In addition to the services as well as construction projects, the lead time traditionally has had an important role in fabrication or production/manufacturing operations. In the production situation, an order is placed considering the lead time so that the item is available on time or the concerned activity is completed on time. Such activities may include:

(i) Procurement of input items/raw materials
(ii) Inbound logistics
(iii) Production of components
(iv) Quality test/inspection
(v) Subassemblies
(vi) Final assembly leading to the finished product
(vii) Final packaging
(viii) Outbound logistics

Now lead time's role is explained for these functions/activities.

4.1.1 Procurement

As shown in Figure 4.3, a production organization can procure certain input items or raw material from a vendor/supply organization/supplier.

For instance, if it takes two weeks to get the input item after placing an order, the procurement lead time is two weeks.

Example 4.1

In case of L.P.G. cylinder fabrication, the following main components are generally subcontracted or procured:

(i) Foot ring
(ii) Valve

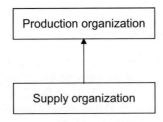

Figure 4.3 Procurement from the supply organization

(iii) Valve protection ring
(iv) Bung

For the L.P.G. cylinder, a foot ring is used as a stand and is welded to the main cylinder. A brass valve is used to act as an outlet for the L.P.G. cylinder with the help of a regulator. The valve protection ring is used for the purpose of protecting the valve from any damage during the handling of the cylinder. The bung is welded to the upper portion of the cylinder and has internal threads. This is a forged steel component, and the valve which has external threads is tightened over it with the help of a torque wrench.

For each component, the lead time should be precisely estimated and an order should be released at a proper time so that the component is available when needed. Lead time estimation may depend on factors such as:

 (i) Production capacity of the supply organization
 (ii) Stock normally available with the supplier
(iii) Previous experience concerning the lead time
(iv) Distance between supplier and buyer locations
 (v) Weightage given by the supply organization to this particular order
(vi) Relationship with the supplier

Precise estimation of lead time helps a lot in overall procurement planning. Generally speaking, the effects of estimation of lead time are shown in Figure 4.4. When it is estimated on the shorter side, there may be a shortage of a particular component and it is may not be available at the time of need. On the other hand, when the lead time is estimated on the higher side, the particular component is available much earlier than the time of need and unnecessary inventory is carried for a certain period of time.

4.1.2 Inbound logistics

As shown in Figure 4.5, inbound logistics refers to the activities pertaining to the transportation of input items/raw materials from the supply organization to the production/buyer organization.

100

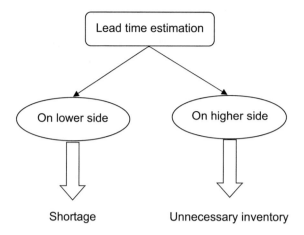

Figure 4.4 Effects of estimation of lead time

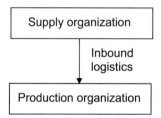

Figure 4.5 Inbound logistics

Related activities may include:

(i) Arrival of the trucks at the supply organization
(ii) Loading the truck
(iii) Transportation along with intermediate halt
(iv) Arrival of the truck at the production organization
(v) Unloading the truck

Such activities need to be studied carefully in order to estimate the lead time and, further, a reduction in it. Additionally, the related factors are as follows:

(i) Who owns the logistics activity? Is it the supplier/buyer, or is it outsourced?
(ii) At what time does the vehicle movement happen? Is it during the day or night? What is the traffic situation during that time?

(iii) Is there any role of rail, waterways, or air, in addition to road transport? Or is it a combination?

(iv) Where does an intermediate halt happen? What are the driver habits/behaviours? What are the problems a driver faces?

4.1.3 Production

The time associated with the manufacturing activity after placing an order for production can relate to the concerned lead time.

Example 4.2

Hot rolled mild steel sheets of 3.15 mm thickness are used as a raw material/input item for production of L.P.G. cylinders. The following main production activities are carried out:

(i) The shearing machine is used to form square pieces from the input item.

(ii) The circle-cutting machine is run to form circles from the square sheet.

(iii) The hydraulic press is employed to make halves from the circles that were cut before.

(iv) One half is welded with a bung after creating an appropriate hole on the top portion.

(v) Another half is welded with a foot ring at appropriate places on the lower portion.

(vi) The two halves thus obtained are welded with the use of a submerged arc welding machine.

(vii) Heat treatment is done for stress relieving.

(viii) After the shot blasting operation, metallizing is done with the help of zinc wire to make the surface suitable for further operations and also to make it corrosion-resistant.

(ix) Finally, painting is performed first with an undercoat of primer and then the finishing layer of synthetic paint.

Observation of these production processes will lead towards an estimation of lead time taken by the cylinder after release of the order. Micro details will lead towards individual components/subcomponents of lead time for further refinement/improvement.

4.1.4 Quality inspection

Quality inspection is necessary at various stages of production activity. These might include:

(i) Raw material processing stage

(ii) Work-in-process item

(iii) Finished product
(iv) Packaging stage

Detection of any defects at an early stage is always preferred so that further processing costs may be avoided or reduced. The costs may relate to production or avoidable material handling.

Similarly, while procuring the input items or components, a certain level of inspection may be needed. This might be at the supplier location or after arrival of the items at the buyer location, depending on the specific case. Factors influencing lead time related to the quality test/inspection are represented in Figure 4.6.

Depending on the product, either 100% inspection may be necessary or a sampling inspection may be enough. Each and every product in the lot or batch is examined in the situation of 100% inspection. This might take a lot of time, affecting the lead time on the higher side. However, a few

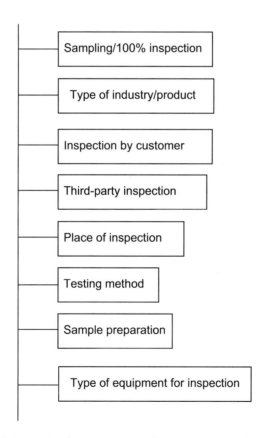

Figure 4.6 Lead time–related aspects concerning quality inspection

samples may be chosen from the whole lot in case of the sampling inspection, and a lot may face the following situations on the basis of those few samples:

(i) Lot is accepted
(ii) Lot is rejected

Since only a few samples are tested/inspected, sampling is less costly and comparatively less time may be consumed. This may contribute towards shorter lead time relatively in the usual case of acceptance.

Another aspect is related to the type of industry/product. In the case of the heavy manufacturing industry, the products might be in the form of heavy machines/equipment (of higher capacity) such as:

(i) Steam turbine
(ii) Transformer
(iii) Generator set

One hundred percent inspection or testing might be needed in the case of final assembly/subassembly among other critical sets of items.

On the other hand, in the case of the light manufacturing industry, sampling inspection may be adopted depending on the specific product. However, on the basis of the product or its specific application, certain types of tests may come under sampling inspection, and 100% inspection may be needed concerning essential/critical tests.

In some cases, inspection by the customer company representative is the norm. This may include inspection of either the finished product or various important stages of production along with the final stage. The associated lead time may concern activities such as the following:

(i) Make the finished component/subassembly/final product ready for inspection.
(ii) Invite the customer on a suitable date and time.
(iii) Arrival of the customer and visit of the factory premises for stage-wise/final inspection.
(iv) Acceptance/suggestion for modification.

In case of acceptance, the producer can go ahead for the next process. Otherwise, they have to rework. If it is a minor rework, it can be done immediately to the satisfaction of the customer. Otherwise, all the previously mentioned steps, that is, (i) to (iv), are repeated and approval of the customer company is taken on some other date and time.

Similarly, in the desired third-party inspection, these steps are followed. Instead of the customer being invited for inspection purposes, the third party such as the authorized representative of the relevant bureau for maintaining quality standards might be invited. An associated lead time should be estimated accordingly.

The place of inspection may relate to the location within the factory premises. In some cases, inspection happens on the job and the inspector goes to the shop floor. However, in certain scenarios, samples are picked up and these are taken to a centralized place within the facility for inspection purposes. Occasionally, the inspection also happens outside the factory premises at some other location, which may be far away, in respect to a suitable facility or available authority. Generally speaking, the place of inspection within the factory depends on aspects such as:

  (i) Type and nature of product/component
 (ii) Weight and size of the product/component
(iii) Criticality of inspection
 (iv) Sampling/100% inspection
  (v) Needed special environment for inspection
 (vi) Type of facility needed for inspection
(vii) Stationary or mobile facility
(viii) Handheld device for inspection

As far as the testing method is concerned, visual examination is enough in certain cases, which takes relatively little time. However, destructive testing may be necessary in other situations concerning the selected sample. This requires a standard facility with provision for precise measurement under specific supervision, which affects the lead time accordingly.

Sample preparation is necessary in order to make it suitable for the intended testing/inspection. Depending on the inspection/testing method and also the product, one or more aspects might be relevant, such as:

  (i) Degreasing
 (ii) Cleaning
(iii) Drying
 (iv) Cutting and filing
  (v) Grinding

In the context of associated time, the type of equipment may relate to:

 (i) Setup time
(ii) Operational or processing time

Lead time may be estimated after recording specific setup time for the inspection or testing equipment. Additionally, the time taken by the equipment for processing or testing the sample may be considered.

4.1.5 Subassembly and final assembly

A final assembly is composed of two or more subassemblies, as shown in Figure 4.7.

In the context of lead time, the following aspects are relevant:

(i) Product design
(ii) Process design

For a similar product design, the associated time may be influenced by a change in the process design. Process design is also related to the postponement or degree of postponement. However, product design is also related to the modularization or degree of modularization. A module is composed of one or more components. These aspects need to be studied thoroughly in order to examine the lead time and any potential lead time reduction.

4.1.6 Final packaging

The role of packaging lies in an ease of handling and safety of product during transit. Scratches should not appear on the product surface during transit/handling, and also it should not get otherwise damaged. In order to achieve this objective, the packaging material should be carefully selected. Final packaging before transportation is affected by factors such as:

(i)   Type and nature of product
(ii) Size and shape of the product
(iii) Material of the product
(iv) Mode of transport

Additionally, the following should be kept in mind:

(i) How many sharp corners appear in the product?
(ii) How many protruding parts are visible in the product?

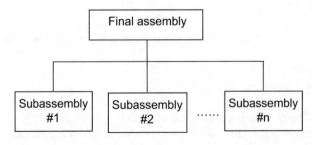

Figure 4.7 Assembly

Care should be taken while packaging so that the sharp corners and protruding parts, among other portions, are not damaged during transit or product handling. An associated time for packaging should be included for further analysis.

4.1.7 Outbound logistics

As shown in Figure 4.8, outbound logistics refers to the activities pertaining to the transportation of finished products towards downstream locations. The downstream locations might be:

(i) Warehouses
(ii) Distribution centres
(iii) Customer companies
(iv) Wholesalers
(v) Retailers
(vi) Consumers

Related activities may include:

(i) Arrival of the trucks at the production organization
(ii) Loading the truck
(iii) Transportation along with intermediate halts
(iv) Arrival of the truck at downstream locations
(v) Unloading the truck

Such activities need to be studied carefully in order to estimate the lead time and further reduction in it. Additionally, related factors are as follows:

(i) Who owns the logistics activity? Is it the production organization/downstream company, or is it outsourced?
(ii) At what time does the vehicle movement happen? Is it during the day or night? What is the traffic situation during that time?

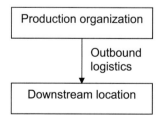

Figure 4.8 Outbound logistics

(iii) Is there any role of rail, waterways, or air, in addition to the road transport? Or is it a combination?

(iv) Where does an intermediate halt happen? What are the driver habits/behaviours? What are the problems a driver faces?

4.2 Existing lead time analysis

Existing lead time needs to be understood and analyzed properly for suggesting ways to reduce it. In order to provide consultancy in this area, it is also necessary to select a few significant types of product from many types being manufactured by the company. This is because a focused approach for recording, tracking, and analyzing can be feasible for a select few types of product. Some of the following factors may be relevant for a particular case concerning the selection of products:

(i) Significance of the customer
(ii) Value of the product
(iii) Profitability of the product
(iv) Contribution of the range of items towards revenue
(v) Problematic range of items in terms of delays in completion
(vi) Effects of relatively longer lead time in terms of customer dissatisfaction and also any penalty imposed by the customer organization in certain cases
(vii) Effects of relatively longer lead time in terms of costs, space, and disruptions in the planned schedule

After selection of an important range of products, time taken in various processes/activities are analyzed to know the existing scenario. In order to analyze the lead time, it is very necessary to understand the processes involved in procurement, production, material handling, and design/planning, among others.

Example 4.3

A wide range of transformers are produced by an organization. These include:

(i) Rectifier transformer
(ii) Locomotive transformer
(iii) Furnace transformer
(iv) Trackside transformer
(v) Power transformer

The organization wants to reduce its lead time. After mutual discussion, a consultancy team focused on the following types of transformers:

(i) 220 KV, 3Ø, 100 MVA
(ii) 220 KV, 3Ø, 200 MVA

(iii) 132 KV, 3Ø, 50 MVA
(iv) 400 KV, 3Ø, 315 MVA
 (v) 400 KV, 1Ø, 105 MVA

These represent their make-to-order production environment suitably. Depending on multiple factors such as total time taken, significance of 3Ø transformers, range of KV and MVA, revenue generation, customer significance, and profitability, these types of transformers are selected for an overall lead time focus.

A necessary step is to understand the processes involved. Significant processes are shown in Figure 4.9 in sequence.

The planning process takes into consideration the feedback of the marketing division concerning the customer orders, and a sales plan is generated. After prioritizing the orders, month-wise scheduling is done, and a production plan is also generated. These plans are circulated to:

 (i) Design and drawing
(ii) Procurement
(iii) Production

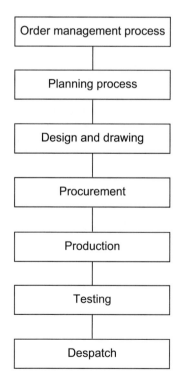

Figure 4.9 Various processes

Each process takes its own time for necessary preparation and action. As per the mechanical/manufacturing design (and also electrical design), the relevant bill of materials is finalized and, accordingly, the procurement process of various items including raw materials is initiated. After the release of necessary items from the stores, the production process starts. This begins with the winding of transformers. Various production processes are as follows:

(i) Winding
(ii) Single phase assembly
(iii) Oven
(iv) Core coil assembly
(v) Connection
(vi) Tanking

After production processes, the transformer is tested finally. It is dismantled and packed and finally dispatched. Now a few important processes are discussed in detail considering the lead time or cycle time objective.

Considering the order management process, certain activities are as follows:

(i) Verifying details of the letter of intent or order
(ii) Contract review
(iii) Creation of order in the system

Table 4.1 may be useful for analyzing the time.

It may be observed that certain manual content exists in the verification of the technical as well as commercial bid with the letter of intent.

After a careful study of the schedule prepared by the planning process and its comparison from the actual performance, it has been observed that there is a certain deviation. However, elaborate information concerning the deviation details is not being captured. The planning process is observed not to have adequate human resources.

The design and drawing process takes one to two months presently for one design. It is also observed that the advanced design software is not being used. Almost one week is consumed by this function to create packaging and the shipping list. After preparing the drawing, an approval of the customer

Table 4.1 Observed time in the order management

Activity	Observed or recorded time
(i)	*(ii)*

Table 4.2 Observed lead time for key components/items

S. No.	Item	Observed lead time

Table 4.3 Actual days taken by the production process

Sales order	Process description	Actual start date	Actual finish date	Actual days taken

is needed. In many cases, more than the three weeks are consumed in this activity, and there is significant scope for reduction in time.

The procurement process also includes an effective coordination with different vendors. Existing lead time can be recorded, as shown in Table 4.2, for certain key items/components.

In the production process, winding is the first important activity. An observation is as follows:

Out of the two workers, one leaves the workstation/job because of the unavailable input item/raw material or the need to discuss some issue with the supervisor. Owing to this, the winding cycle time can increase.

Generally speaking, actual time for each activity should be recorded. While studying the gap between planned and actual time, the winding activity was found to have the maximum gap, that is, on the order of five weeks on an average concerning five specific types of transformers mentioned earlier. Actual days taken for each process can be recorded, as shown in Table 4.3.

Actual days taken can be obtained from the system considering the actual:

(i) Finish date
(ii) Start date

In a similar manner, stage-wise testing and dispatch details can be captured in appropriate tabular form so that a comparison can be made between actual time spent and the planned time.

4.3 Lead time reduction

After understanding the existing process and recording the present lead time at various stages, opportunities should be explored to reduce the present lead time.

Example 4.4

In the previous example, the processes related to the transformer manufacturing industry are discussed along with the existing lead time analysis. Now the next step is to explore the opportunities for reducing the time taken so that suitable suggestions for modification can be offered.

As was mentioned before, significant processes are as follows:

(i) Order management process
(ii) Planning process
(iii) Design and drawing
(iv) Procurement
(v) Production along with stage-wise inspection/testing
(vi) Dispatch

Concerning the order management process, verification of the technical as well as commercial bid with the letter of intent is an important activity among others. In order to project the time reduction, Table 4.4 may be useful.

For example, creation of the standard template has the potential to reduce the time for verification activity to almost 50%. In a similar manner, a thorough study for the work content in significant activities can lead to projecting the overall reduction in time.

Currently the planning process incorporates the inputs/suggestions concerning the processes from the remaining sections, and then a schedule is prepared by the planning section. However, it has been observed that the remaining sections are finding it difficult to complete the process in the time span suggested by them. Therefore, a deviation exists from the planned performance in terms of time taken. However, elaborate information concerning the deviation details is not being captured. If this is done with the removal of the root cause of the problems, an achievable plan can be created by the planning process and frequent rescheduling can be avoided, thus reducing the cycle time associated with the planning process. Such an expected reduction in time can go to the order of approximately four days. However, in order to achieve this effectively, adequate human resources may be necessary in the planning division. This is because of associated work concerning standard time estimates among other things.

Table 4.4 Time reduction in the order management

Activity (i)	Observed or recorded time (ii)	Expected time (iii)	Projected reduction (ii)–(iii)

Concerning the design and drawing process, there is significant potential for reduction in the lead time by one to two weeks with the use of advanced design software. Furthermore, in both the mechanical and electrical design, there is certain scope for parallel design activity contributing towards lead time reduction. Additionally, almost one week is consumed in order to create packaging and shipping lists. It may be possible for the dispatch function to do this task.

Procurement lead time can be analyzed with the help of Table 4.5.

If the observed lead time is more than what is planned, then the difference is positive and the 'remarks' column should be filled with the reasons for delay. On the other hand, if the observed lead time is less than that planned, then the planned lead time itself can be modified in the system. Such modification should be made only after ensuring that the previously planned time was overestimated and a suitable correction can be made.

An attempt should also be made by the procurement division to prevent the reasons for delay. Such prevention is expected to lead towards potential time reduction in purchase. These reasons may include:

(i) Frequent design changes and subsequent communication to vendors resulting in delay
(ii) Lack of communication/coordination with the design activity
(iii) Lack of communication/coordination with the vendors
(iv) Input item rejection in some cases
(v) Development of vendors
(vi) Vendor rating and fair analysis

Table 4.5 Lead time analysis for key components/items

Item (i)	Observed lead time (ii)	Planned lead time (iii)	Difference (ii)–(iii)	Remarks

Table 4.6 Deviation analysis for production and dispatch

Sales order	Process description	Actual start date	Actual finish date	Actual days taken (a)	Planned days (b)	Deviation (a)–(b)	Remarks

For the production and dispatch activities, Table 4.6 is useful for deviation analysis.

As mentioned earlier, actual days taken can be obtained considering start and finish date and can be compared with the planned days. Reasons for delay may be entered in the 'remarks' column for corrective action. This results in a potential reduction in the associated time concerning production activities and dispatch.

Similarly, stage-wise inspection and testing are performed and any delay can be analyzed. These delays might happen because of:

(i) Producing organization
(ii) Customer organization
(iii) Weather
(iv) Infrastructural issues

The producing organization may not have resources pertaining to the desired facility available for newly introduced tests. Or the competent human resource may not be available on the day when customer desires to have a joint inspection. There might be administrative delays in arranging for a joint inspection by producer and customer representatives. Weather may not be favourable for certain tests, or it may be difficult to create an appropriate environment for intended tests. Also from the customer side, it might be difficult to reach the site for inspection because of rain/weather or there might be infrastructural issues. Or the competent customer representative may not be available on the proposed date.

Customer inspection is also necessary at certain stages, and better communication and coordination with the customer in this make-to-order environment can result in minimization of delays, among other avoidable reasons.

4.4 Interdepartmental conflicts

In the previous section, customer inspection at the various stages was discussed. However in certain cases, customer company priority may also change, particularly in a make-to-order scenario, because of a considerably long total lead time of a few months to many months. For example, the customer plans to receive the transformer after six months and accordingly places an order. But they realize after three months that the product will remain idle for next two months in case of the scheduled receipt. It is now in the interest of the customer to delay the completion. Such a scenario relates to the interface of the customer and the producing company. However, within the manufacturing or producing company, there are also multiple departments and interdepartmental conflicts happen in the context of lead time. Various departments/functions are shown in Figure 4.10.

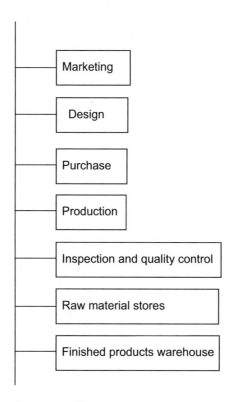

Figure 4.10 Various departments/functions

4.4.1 Marketing and design

The marketing function plays an important role in generating the requirements of customers and communicating them to the organization. Briefly speaking, the marketing function might communicate the requirement related to the product (for example, a transformer) to the design section, as shown in Figure 4.11.

Design and drawing are prepared accordingly, and customer approval may be needed in coordination with marketing. However, the customer company may feel that the requirements are not fully understood, and there are delays in final approval until the customer is satisfied. A certain level of conflict may occur within the manufacturing organization related to the design and marketing departments, such as which function is more responsible for delays in the organization.

4.4.2 Marketing and production

The job of the marketing department includes taking orders from the customer. Such orders are communicated to the production department either through

115

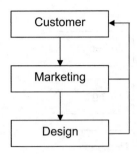

Figure 4.11 Marketing and design communication

design/planning, as mentioned before, or directly. In the case in which it is directly communicated to the production, there is usually a standard product being manufactured repeatedly and additionally fresh design efforts are not needed. In a situation in which lead time plays an important role, the marketing division may reduce it as per the customer requirement. As the lead time is reduced, there is a chance of quoting a higher price and the marketing function can take the credit for generating higher revenue. Since revenue is usually the performance criterion for this function, higher revenue generation with less effort goes in favour of the marketing department. However, if production has to complete the task in a shorter time than usual, such an offered excessively shorter lead time does not go in favour of the production section. Thus, the chance of inter-departmental conflict between marketing and production appears.

4.4.3 Purchase and production

As per the production plan, among other information, purchase of the components and input items usually happens. However, if the production plan frequently changes, then the purchase function is affected negatively. The reasons for frequent changes in production plan are provided in Figure 4.12. Customer order changes are of the following types:

(i) Customer requirement changes in terms of quantity, and accordingly purchasing requirements for input items also change.
(ii) Customer requirement changes in terms of quality or specification, and accordingly purchasing plan is affected.
(iii) Customer order changes in terms of both quality and quantity.

The following situations may emerge concerning the priority of the order:

(i) Sometimes an urgent order may appear because of either the value of the order or the significant customer value. In such a case, the priority may change.

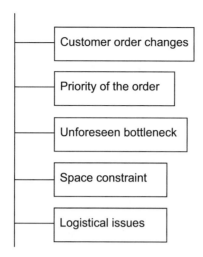

Figure 4.12 Reasons for changes in the production plan

(ii) Sometimes an existing order gets stuck midway, for example, because of longer delays such as a customer inspection problem. Instead of resources being idle, another order may proceed if it is possible.

There are also situations of unforeseen bottlenecks. For instance, one plant out of seven plants is shut down because of reasons such as:

(i) Severe environmental issues such as heavy rains/storm
(ii) Strike

In the case of a centralized purchase, the economies of scale concerning purchase may not be available partially because of the lower overall production requirement for a certain period.

Space constraints might happen owing to:

(i) A heavy product/subassembly gets stuck at a certain stage for processing/inspection. Because of that work-in-process, inventory accumulates prior to that stage leading to a kind of 'traffic jam'.
(ii) In a serial production case, there may not be space to keep the output of one facility beyond a certain limit if the next facility is facing a major maintenance problem.

Logistical issues may pertain to internal as well as external logistics. Material handling within the plant can become an issue because either a crane is not working or it cannot lift certain item because of a 'traffic jam' although the crane is in working condition.

4.4.4 Purchase and inspection

After the standard purchasing procedure, a lot or batch of input items/ raw materials arrives in the organization. A certain level of inspection is needed for subsequent record keeping. It may also be desirable to know whether:

(i) A lot is accepted
(ii) A lot is rejected
(iii) A rework is required before acceptance

Lead time taken by the inspection and quality control functions has an implication for record keeping and further necessary action by the purchasing department.

4.4.5 Production and raw material stores

Various raw materials and input items are stored for release to the production department from time to time. On some occasions, the production department wants the release of input items for another order because one order got stuck in the plant for variety of reasons, as mentioned earlier. However, raw material inventory analysis might reveal that there is a chance of the average inventory going up within the organization because input items are taking more time than usual for completion of orders.

4.4.6 Finished products warehouse and marketing

In many instances, the marketing division plays an important/coordination role in scheduled dispatches from the finished products warehouse, outbound logistics, and customer receipts. Longer lead time may be on account of:

(i) Packaging issues
(ii) Unavailability of transporting medium
(iii) Customer issues

In the case of delays, a finished products warehouse may not have enough space for incoming final products from the factory.

Different types of interactions have been described. The management should pay attention to resolve the differences of opinions and objectives, and an effort should be made to eliminate or reduce interdepartmental conflicts presently found in the organization.

Exercises

1 What do you understand by lead time? Explain it in the context of:

(i) Service operations
(ii) Production operations

2 Discuss the role of lead time in the following situations:

(i) Catering services
(ii) House building
(iii) Publishing
(iv) Garment manufacturing
(v) Agricultural products
(vi) Shelf life
(vii) Production

3 Explain how the related components of lead time in the context of house building may include:

(i) Selection of the location
(ii) Procurement of the land
(iii) Procurement of related building materials at various stages
(iv) Construction of the house
(v) Finishing and electricity fitting
(vi) Final handing over/taking over

4 In the case of L.P.G. cylinder fabrication, the following main components are generally subcontracted or procured:

(i) Foot ring
(ii) Valve
(iii) Valve protection ring
(iv) Bung

For the L.P.G. cylinder, a foot ring is used as a stand and is welded to the main cylinder. A brass valve is used to act as an outlet for L.P.G. with the help of a regulator. A valve protection ring is used for the purpose of protecting the valve from any damage during the handling of the cylinder. The bung is welded to the upper portion of the cylinder and has internal threads. This is a forged steel component and the valve, which has external threads, is tightened over it with the help of a torque wrench.

Foreach component, the lead time should be precisely estimated and an order should be released at proper time so that the component is available when needed.

Elaborate how lead time estimation may depend on factors such as:

(i) Production capacity of the supply organization
(ii) Stock normally available with the supplier

(iii) Previous experience concerning the lead time

(iv) Distance between supplier and buyer locations

 (v) Weightage given by the supply organization to this particular order

(vi) Relationship with the supplier

5 Describe what happens when lead time estimation is on:

 (i) Shorter side

(ii) Longer side

6 Inbound logistics refers to the activities pertaining to the transportation of input items/raw materials from the supply organization to the production/buyer organization. Explain the related activities that may include:

  (i) Arrival of the trucks at the supply organization

 (ii) Loading the truck

(iii) Transportation along with intermediate halt

(iv) Arrival of the truck at the production organization

 (v) Unloading the truck

7 Discuss why it is necessary in the context of lead time to consider the following related factors:

  (i) Who owns the logistics activity? Is it the supplier/buyer, or is it outsourced?

 (ii) At what time does the vehicle movement happen? Is it during the day or night? What is the traffic situation during that time?

(iii) Is there any role of rail, waterways, or air, in addition to the road transport? Or is it a combination?

(iv) Where does an intermediate halt happen?

 (v) What are the driver habits/behaviours?

(vi) What are the problems a driver faces?

8 The time associated with the manufacturing activity after placing an order for production can relate to the lead time. Comment on the following:

Observation of production processes will lead towards an estimation of lead time taken by the product after release of the order. Micro details will lead towards individual components/subcomponents of lead time for further refinement/improvement.

9 Explain the lead time–related aspects concerning quality inspection, such as:

  (i) Sampling

 (ii) 100% inspection

(iii) Type of industry

(iv) Type of product

 (v) Customer inspection

(vi) Third-party inspection

(vii) Place of inspection

(viii) Testing method
(ix) Sample preparation
(x) Type of equipment for inspection

10 In some cases, inspection by the customer company representative is the norm. This may include either the finished product or various important stages of production along with the final stage. Elaborate how the associated lead time may concern activities such as the following:

(i) Make the finished component/subassembly/final product ready for inspection.
(ii) Invite the customer on a suitable date and time.
(iii) Arrival of the customer and visit of the factory premises for stage-wise/final inspection.
(iv) Acceptance/suggestion for modification.

11 Describe how the place of inspection within the factory depends on the following aspects:

(i) Type and nature of product/component
(ii) Weight and size of the product/component
(iii) Criticality of inspection
(iv) Sampling/100% inspection
(v) Needed special environment for inspection
(vi) Type of facility needed for inspection
(vii) Stationary or mobile facility
(viii) Handheld device for inspection

12 Sample preparation is necessary in order to make it suitable for the intended testing/inspection. Depending on the inspection/testing method and also the product, discuss how one or more aspects might be relevant, such as:

(i) Degreasing
(ii) Cleaning
(iii) Drying
(iv) Cutting and filing
(v) Grinding

13 In the context of associated time, why might the type of equipment relate to the following?

(i) Setup time
(ii) Operational or processing time

14 With reference to lead time, why are the following aspects relevant?

(i) Product design
(ii) Process design

15 Explain how final packaging before transportation is affected by the following factors:

(i) Type and nature of the product
(ii) Size and shape of the product
(iii) Material of the product
(iv) Mode of transport

16 With reference to packaging, why should the following be kept in mind?

(i) How many sharp corners appear in the product?
(ii) How many protruding parts are visible in the product?

17 Outbound logistics refers to the activities pertaining to the transportation of finished products towards downstream locations. In this context, describe the downstream locations such as:

(i) Warehouses
(ii) Distribution centres
(iii) Customer companies
(iv) Wholesalers
(v) Retailers
(vi) Consumers

18 Existing lead time needs to be understood and analyzed properly for suggesting ways to reduce it. In order to provide consultancy in this area, it is also necessary to select a few significant types of product from many types being manufactured by the company. Discuss how some of the following factors may be relevant for a certain case concerning the selection of products:

(i) Significance of the customer
(ii) Value of the product
(iii) Profitability of the product
(iv) Contribution of the range of items towards revenue
(v) Problematic range of items in terms of delays in completion
(vi) Effects of relatively longer lead time in terms of customer dissatisfaction and also any penalty imposed by the customer organization in certain cases
(vii) Effects of relatively longer lead time in terms of costs, space, and disruptions in the planned schedule.

19 A wide range of transformers are produced by an organization. These include:

(i) Rectifier transformer
(ii) Locomotive transformer
(iii) Furnace transformer
(iv) Trackside transformer
(v) Power transformer

The organization wants to reduce its lead time. A necessary step is to understand the processes involved. In this context, explain the significant processes such as:

   (i) Order management process
  (ii) Planning process
 (iii) Design and drawing
 (iv) Procurement
  (v) Production
 (vi) Testing
(vii) Dispatch

20 Considering the order management process, certain activities are as follows:

  (i) Verifying details of the letter of intent or order
 (ii) Contract review
(iii) Creation of order in the system

In order to analyze the time taken for each activity, elaborate how the following may be useful:

Activity	Observed or recorded time
(i)	*(ii)*

21 The procurement process also includes effective coordination with different vendors. Existing lead time can be recorded for certain key items/components. Comment on the application of the following:

S. No.	Item	Observed lead time

22 In the production process, winding is the first important activity. An observation is as follows:

Out of the two workers, one leaves the workstation/job because of an unavailable input item/raw material or the need to discuss some issue with the supervisor. Owing to this, the winding cycle time can increase.

    Generally speaking, actual time for each activity should be recorded. Comment on the utility of the following:

Sales order	Process description	Actual start date	Actual finish date	Actual days taken

23 Concerning the order management process, verification of the technical as well as commercial bid with the letter of intent is an important activity, among others. In order to project the time reduction, explain how the following may be useful.

Activity (i)	Observed or recorded time (ii)	Expected time (iii)	Projected reduction (ii)–(iii)

24 An organization procures a wide variety of materials/items for various activities, such as production of components, subassembly, final assembly, and packaging. In the context of procurement lead time, elaborate how it can be analyzed with the help of the following:

Item (i)	Observed lead time (ii)	Planned lead time (iii)	Difference (ii)–(iii)	Remarks

25 An attempt should also be made by the procurement division to prevent the reasons for delay. Such prevention is expected to lead towards potential time reduction in the purchase. Discuss the reasons that may include:

 (i) Frequent design changes and subsequent communication to vendors resulting in delay
 (ii) Lack of communication/coordination with the design activity
 (iii) Lack of communication/coordination with the vendors
 (iv) Input item rejection in some cases
 (v) Development of vendors
 (vi) Vendor rating and fair analysis

26 For the production and dispatch activities, elaborate how the following
is helpful for deviation analysis.

Sales order	Process description	Actual start date	Actual finish date	Actual days taken (a)	Planned days (b)	Deviation (a)–(b)	Remarks

27 Stage-wise inspection and testing are also performed, and any delay can
be analyzed. With reference to this, comment how these delays might happen because of:

(i) Producing organization
(ii) Customer organization
(iii) Weather
(iv) Infrastructural issues

28 Within the manufacturing or producing company, there are multiple
departments and interdepartmental conflicts happen in the context of
lead time. For this purpose, consider the following departments:

(i) Marketing
(ii) Design
(iii) Purchase
(iv) Production
(v) Inspection and quality control
(vi) Raw material stores
(vii) Finished products warehouse

And describe interdepartmental conflicts such as those between:

(i) Marketing and design
(ii) Marketing and production
(iii) Purchase and production
(iv) Purchase and inspection
(v) Production and raw material stores
(vi) Finished products warehouse and marketing

29 Comment on the customer order changes that are of the following types:

(i) Customer requirement changes in terms of quantity
(ii) Customer requirement changes in terms of quality or specification

(iii) Customer order changes in terms of both quality and quantity

30 Comment on the following situations that may emerge concerning the priority of an order:

(i) Sometimes an urgent order may appear because of either the value of the order or the significant customer value. In such a case, the priority may change.

(ii) Sometimes an existing order gets stuck midway, for example, because of longer delays such as a customer inspection problem. Instead of resources being idle, another order may proceed if it is possible.

31 Comment on the longer lead time that may be on account of:

(i) Packaging issues
(ii) Unavailability of transporting medium
(iii) Customer issues

5

OUTSOURCING CONSIDERATION

Almost every organization, whether industrial or business, faces the problem of outsourcing. It has to decide whether a particular activity under consideration should be finally outsourced. This chapter provides a basic understanding in this area so that the reader becomes familiar with the ample scope of industrial consultancy in this specific field. Additionally, a number of examples are discussed for practical exposure. Cases are mentioned considering steel tube production and the L.P.G. cylinder manufacturing industry. The outsourcing relationship between buyer and supplier is described specifically, including the factors influencing it.

An organization has several tasks/activities to do, and it is not possible to do all of them within the boundaries of the organization. Since such aspects have strategic as well as operational implications, these should be appropriately covered and discussed. If a certain activity including a product or service is sourced from outside, then it is termed as 'outsourcing'. The following terms are used in this context as these have a more or less similar meaning: (i) purchase or buy; (ii) externalizing/externalize; and (iii) outsourcing/outsource.

In a case in which an activity is completed within the organization itself, all the associated resources need to be arranged within the related boundaries. If a certain activity is not outsourced, then the following terms have a more or less similar meaning: (i) make or produce; (ii) internalizing/internalize; and (iii) insourcing/insource.

As shown in Figure 5.1, an activity is under consideration for outsourcing.

Presently, many activities are done by an organization, represented by 'Δ'. An activity represented by 'O' is under consideration for outsourcing. However, analysis is needed to decide whether this activity should be outsourced or whether the present practice of making/manufacturing/producing/doing it within the organization is better. Such an analysis is necessary to prevent failure at a later stage or to reduce the possibility of failure concerning the decision.

On the other hand, an activity 'I', as shown in Figure 5.2, is presently being outsourced; that is, it is externalized or purchased from outside.

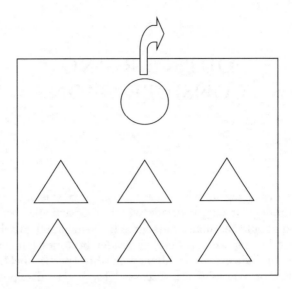

Figure 5.1 Activity 'O' under consideration

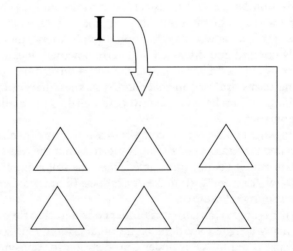

Figure 5.2 Activity 'I' under consideration

A decision is to be made whether this activity 'I' should be insourced, that is, whether internalizing/making it within the organization would be better or whether the current practice of outsourcing/purchasing it from outside should continue.

5.1 Basics of outsourcing

Before outsourcing any activity, for example, manufacture of a component, the types of factors to be considered broadly are as follows:

(i) Cost factors
(ii) Non-cost factors

Cost factors alone may not be enough for a final decision, however, and certain non-cost factors also need to be taken into consideration in many cases. Therefore, a combination of these factors may be more appropriate in order to finalize the decision and also visualize the outcome or foresee an implication of any decision making, that is, either insourcing or outsourcing. Relevant cost factors are usually be the first step for listing, estimating, and accounting.

The cost factors should be viewed from two sides:

(i) Associated cost while insourcing
(ii) Associated cost while outsourcing

5.1.1 Associated cost while insourcing

Associated cost while insourcing relates to the expenditure incurred when producing a product or service within the house in its entirety. The associated cost while outsourcing relates to the expenditure in totality when purchasing a product or service from outside and receiving it in the company for furthermore processing.

Factors related to the associated cost while insourcing are provided in Figure 5.3.

Although raw material purchase and transportation costs fluctuate, these need to be estimated to arrive at the procurement cost of input/raw material. Raw material purchase cost depends on the following aspects among others:

(i) Availability
(ii) Quantity to be purchased

Transportation cost for input items depends on the following aspects, among others:

(i) Distance of the source of input items
(ii) Transportation medium being used

Overall, raw material procurement cost may be composed of purchase and transportation costs. If the raw material is not easily available or the availability is less than the requirement for a certain period, then there is a strong

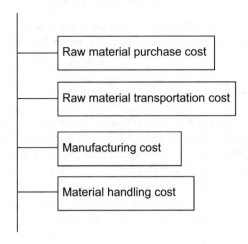

Figure 5.3 Factors for cost while insourcing

possibility of higher purchase cost. On the other hand, when availability is satisfactory, then there is a possibility of discounts on larger quantity purchase. Another component of the overall procurement cost is associated with transportation. In a case in which distance between the source of the input item and the destination is greater, the transportation costs would be relatively higher. Furthermore, this cost also depends on the medium being used, that is, land, water, or air. It is also affected by the type of vehicle, that is, larger or smaller.

After the raw material purchase, the component is manufactured within the organization. Possible scenarios should be kept in mind while analyzing because the approach for estimating the relevant manufacturing cost may vary. This basically will depend on:

(i) Availability of machinery
(ii) Non-availability of machinery/fixed assets

These factors, along with other aspects such as major/minor setup, should be included in an estimation of the manufacturing cost. In order to estimate the manufacturing cost, various scenarios are presented in Figure 5.4.

If it is intended to manufacture a component within the house, then the following two situations emerge:

(i) Fixed assets/machinery may not be available. In a normal case, if a certain machine is required to produce a component, then it may be procured and installed. However, in a cases in which a machine or a set of workstations needs a lot of space, then the availability of an area might be a significant problem because of congestion.

130

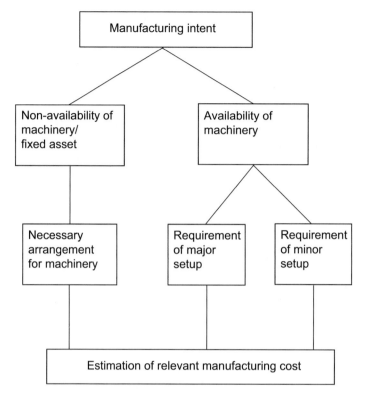

Figure 5.4 Various scenarios for manufacturing

(ii) Machinery is available in the plant and therefore might be utilized to produce the intended component in addition to the existing jobs being processed currently on that machine.

In the situation in which a machine is not available, a necessary arrangement is required. Either an old machine (if available for sale in the market/business) or a new machine may be procured considering the following aspects, among others:

(i) Planning period
(ii) Remaining life of the old machine
(iii) Life of the new machine
(iv) Procurement cost of the old machine
(v) Procurement cost of the new machine

Accordingly, the fixed cost of the machine should be estimated along with the variable cost to produce the component for arriving at the relevant manufacturing cost estimation.

In a situation in which the machine is available in the plant, further activity may be as follows:

(i) Major setup
(ii) Minor setup

As the machine is available, the fixed cost has already been incurred, and therefore accounting for the fixed cost might not be relevant in many cases. However, as the machine is doing some other task currently, there is a need for either major or minor setup for the intended component manufacture. Table 5.1 shows these setup types.

Depending on the setup, time and effort should be accounted for along with the involvement of human resources. This leads to an objective of relevant manufacturing cost estimation including the related setup component as well as actual production cost after the corresponding setup. The quantity to be produced in one setup also plays a role in the relevant cost estimation.

In addition to the manufacturing cost, material handling within the plant should also be studied. Material handling cost specifically pertaining to the component insourced depends on:

(i) Material flow and movement
(ii) Equipment used for handling
(iii) Source of power for the material handling equipment
(iv) Quantity to be handled

Thus, associated cost while insourcing can be estimated considering:

(i) Raw material purchase cost
(ii) Raw material transportation cost
(iii) Manufacturing cost
(iv) Material handling cost

Table 5.1 Major/minor setup

Major setup	Minor setup
(1) Machine needs to be set up significantly	(1) No need for significant machine setup
(2) Considerable machine parameter change with trial run	(2) Minor parameter change without trial run
(3) Work piece setup requires major effort and time	(3) Less effort and time for work piece adjustment
(4) Considerable tooling change	(4) Minor or no tool change

The associated cost while insourcing should be compared with that of outsourcing.

5.1.2 Associated cost while outsourcing

For example, if the manufacture of a component is outsourced, then the total cost while outsourcing should be estimated. Factors related to this estimation are provided in Figure 5.5.

Component purchase cost depends on:

(i) Availability of component/supplier
(ii) Required quantity for that component

If a certain component is not easily available or it is imported, then the purchase cost might be greater. In a case in which an organization requires larger quantities of a component because of greater demand for a finished product, then there is a possibility of a lower purchase cost if the availability is satisfactory. This may be due to better negotiation concerning a contract or offered discounts.

Component transportation cost depends on:

(i) Distance between supplier and buyer location
(ii) Transportation medium being used

In a case in which a supplier company is located far away, the transportation cost may go higher. Such costs also depend on the transportation medium, which may vary from road/truck to railways, among others. Size of the vehicle also influences the transportation cost.

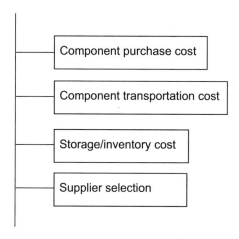

Figure 5.5 Factors for cost while outsourcing

In some cases, storage/inventory cost may also be accounted for. Because of outsourcing, a buyer organization may like to have the components well in advance and store them before actual use. In the case of insourcing, the organization may have control over their operations and can produce at the time of use or just before that. However, when the business follows just-in-time principles and the supplier takes the component directly to the assembly line or arrival happens just-in-time, then the storage/inventory cost can be ignored in outsourcing because of negligible/no storage of components.

If the supplier is easily available or sourcing is possible easily and directly from the market, then the supplier selection might not be a major factor to consider. However, in many cases, a lot of effort is needed for supplier selection and evaluation. This may involve activities such as the following:

(i) Finalize the specification for a component along with other terms and conditions
(ii) Invite the quotation/notice inviting tender
(iii) Tender evaluation
(iv) Supplier selection
(v) Periodic supplier evaluation and review
(vi) Coordination efforts

Thus, the associated cost should be estimated while outsourcing, with the consideration of relevant factors. Now costs concerned with insourcing and outsourcing should be compared, as shown in Figure 5.6, and whether to outsource can be analyzed.

However, a final decision may sometimes not be made on the basis of cost alone. In addition to cost factors, there are certain non-cost factors. Some issues pertaining to such factors are as follows:

(i) If an activity is of critical importance, it may not be outsourced. Rather the company should try to do itself from internal resources. For example, the design activity among others in some organizations might be cited. However, either a company may have appropriate and competent resources or it may not. In the case of the availability of competent resources, it can do the job in the best possible manner or relatively better than the other available enterprises in the market. However, if it is not so, there is a need to develop requisite skills. In order to develop or enhance competence, an organization can pursue:

(a) Suitable software procurement
(b) Training of relevant employees

On the other hand, if a certain activity is not of strategic significance and the company does not have enough resources to do it well, then there is a possibility to outsource it.

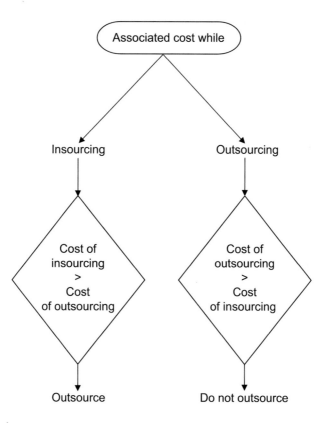

Figure 5.6 Whether to outsource

(ii) While outsourcing an activity, the service provider may know the technical as well as other aspects, and some parties including the service provider and competitors might take the benefit of this situation. It may have harmful effects concerning the business of an organization outsourcing certain activity. Such effects might include:

(a) Lack of coordination/control over the outsourced activity
(b) Supplier becoming the competitor in the case of a high degree of outsourcing

5.2 Outsourcing decision

While making a decision on outsourcing, both cost as well as non-cost factors should be considered. However, in some cases the cost factors may be predominant, and the non-cost factors might be of crucial importance in certain other situations. Such factors might have a strategic dimension also, varying from business to business as well as individual organization to organization.

Example 5.1

A steel tube manufacturing company produces tube/pipe in a variety of:

  (i) Diameters
 (ii) Thicknesses
(iii) Lengths

The immediate input item is cold rolled coil for certain products. Coils are slit into a suitable width, and the appropriate width of the coil is formed into pipe or tube and finally welded and cut to a suitable length. The mentioned input item, that is, those coils, can be procured from outside. However, there is considerable distance between the major supplier company and the buyer, that is, the steel tube manufacturing company. Because of this, the transportation cost is higher. Depending on the thickness of the final product, that is, steel tube, a wide variety of thicknesses for the coil is needed. As shown in Figure 5.7, the company has two options:

(a) Procure a wide variety of thicknesses of coil and directly take the coil to the tube mill as an input item

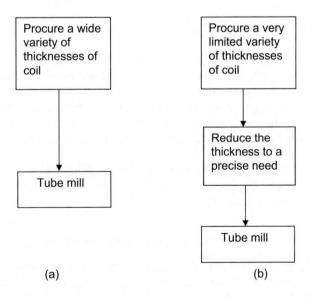

Figure 5.7 Options before the steel tube manufacturing company

(b) Procure very few thicknesses of coil and introduce an intermediate operation for reducing the thickness to the precise need of steel tube

In the case of the first option (a), the degree of outsourcing is very high and since the purchase is for a wide variety of thicknesses, each variety might be in stock for certain quantities. This leads to excessive storage/inventory cost in addition to an increased transportation cost because of the distance between supplier and buyer locations, among other reasons. However, in the case of the second option (b), the degree of outsourcing is reduced by a considerable extent with a certain investment in plant and machinery, that is, the rolling mill. A very small variety of thicknesses is procured from outside, and then the coil thickness is reduced to the precise need at an installed rolling mill adjacent to the tube mill if sufficient space is available. Comparison of both the options is also provided in Table 5.2.

In the present case, option (a) is the existing scenario. While considering all factors, they can switch to option (b) easily because the company has enough space to expand and the rolling mill can be installed adjacent to the tube mill. Output of the rolling mill can be fed as input into the tube mill after slitting to a suitable width of coil. However, a combination of the following factors and analysis (primarily on the basis of cost factors) led the company to decide in favour of option (b):

(i) Cost reduction in terms of storage/inventory
(ii) Cost reduction in terms of purchase and transportation
(iii) Additional production cost and whether it is less than the total cost reduction concerning (i) and (ii) for a specified period in order to provide the potential benefit

Table 5.2 Options for the tube manufacturing company

Option (a)	Option (b)
Purchase of wide variety of thicknesses of coil	Purchase of a very small variety of thicknesses
Higher storage/inventory cost	Lower storage/inventory cost
Higher purchase and transportation costs	Lower purchase and transportation costs
Production cost concerning additional operation for thickness reduction is nil	Production cost concerning additionally introduced operation for thickness reduction is incurred
No requirement for additional space	Additional space is needed for plant and machinery
Additional investment for plant and machinery is nil	Additional investment for plant and machinery

(iv) Level of investment

(v) Payback period for needed investment

(vi) Justification for investment in the context of potential benefit among other aspects

Example 5.2

L.P.G. cylinders are fabricated after welding two halves. In the upper half, a forged steel part called a bung is welded after creating a circular hole on top of the upper half and degreasing this. This part has internal threads for fitting of the brass valve later at the final stage. By using a submerged arc along with a copper-coated mild steel electrode, bung welding is done after fitting it in the hole punched on the upper half. The sequence of this process is shown in Figure 5.8.

The following argument may go in favour of insourcing this component:

(i) Since the L.P.G. cylinder is fabricated out of steel as a major input item and a component made of forged steel also broadly comes under the ferrous metal/alloy category only, it might be possible to insource with certain efforts.

(ii) Although the company does not have machinery such as a forging press currently, the possibility to procure and install the required facility may still be explored.

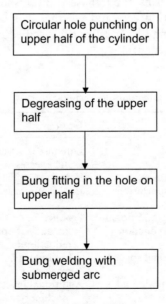

Figure 5.8 Process sequence for bung welding

However, the following reasons may also be given in favour of outsourcing the component:

(i) As the facility is currently not available and internal threads are also to be made on the component, internal thread cutting is an additional operation, among others. Relevant expertise does not seem to be available as of now.

(ii) Creation of this part within the house does not seem to be of strategic importance. It may also not contribute towards a competitive advantage in business.

(iii) Other factories can do the job better, at least presently.

The company under consideration traditionally outsources this component with internal threads mainly on the basis of non-cost factors without rigorous long-term cost analysis.

Example 5.3

A part that is traditionally outsourced by the L.P.G. cylinder manufacturing company is mentioned in the previous example. This part has internal threads and at the end of production processes, a brass valve with external threads is tightened over the mentioned part on the top portion of the cylinder. A sequence of the process for valve fitting is shown in Figure 5.9.

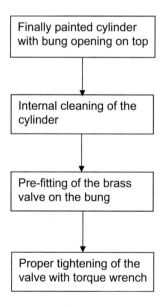

Figure 5.9 Process sequence for valve fitting

The utility of the brass valve lies in its ability to allow the exit of gas and also stoppage, with the help of a regulator fitted on the valve during actual use. The brass valve is also outsourced. A primary reason for this lies in the valve being made of brass. This broadly comes under the non-ferrous category, whereas the major operations and expertise within the company relate to the ferrous category. Under such a scenario, much rationale is not visible in exploring the insourcing case, and the outsourcing of the standard brass valve continues in the company successfully.

Example 5.4

For the L.P.G. cylinder, the foot ring is used as a stand and welded to the lower portion of the cylinder. It is made of a steel sheet, and processes are shown in Figure 5.10.

The sheet is sheared into smaller widths, and those strips are used to further process and make the foot ring. The strip is rolled and welded at the joint to give it a ring-type shape. Depending on the customer company, that is, a particular oil company, either round or oval shaped holes are punched on the periphery of the foot ring. To make the ring more stable and convenient to take the load of cylinder in vertical position, a certain bend is provided to one end of the ring along with small round holes. This end will be the bottommost portion after getting the foot ring welded to the cylinder.

The company has the facility to fabricate foot rings. However, at one point in time, they were indifferent related to insourcing/outsourcing of this ring. For a certain period, they outsourced it. While outsourcing, the following was the experience:

(i) Control of the company over the outsourced operation is lost partially.

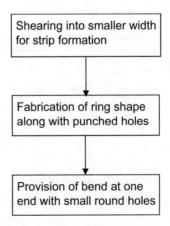

Figure 5.10 Processes for foot ring fabrication

(ii) As the shape of the hole may vary depending on the customer company, there is a need to keep sufficient stock of each type. This results in a higher inventory cost. However, the inventory cost might be lowered comparatively if the relevant hole creation could be postponed. This is possible only when the said operation is not done by the supplier and it is performed by the buyer of the foot ring at a later date within their company depending on the precise demand. But the process is split, the production cost increases relatively, and complete responsibility of the part is not of the supplier.

(iii) Transportation cost is incurred and indirectly is added to the overall procurement cost.

The L.P.G. cylinder manufacturing company under consideration already has the facilities and expertise pertaining to the sheet metal working. After experimenting for a certain period related to the outsourced foot ring, they switched to fabricating it within the company, that is, insourcing. This was also the traditional practice earlier on.

In the wide variety of examples discussed earlier, the decisions are made by the companies on whether to outsource. Generally speaking, such decisions are made on the basis of:

(i) Cost factors
(ii) Non-cost factors
(iii) A combination of cost as well as non-cost factors

In the case of a company about to be launched, an existing scenario pertaining to them may not be available. Therefore, they may weigh both the options of insourcing/outsourcing an activity under consideration. This is on the basis of a variety of factors discussed earlier. In the case of an already operational company, the existing practice and associated features are available to review. In a situation in which they are insourcing a certain activity, a true picture concerning relevant cost and non-cost factors for the existing scenario should be made available. This can be compared with the proposed scenario of outsourcing that includes all relevant factors. After comparison, a suitable decision can be made. In the event of an outsourcing decision, the existing facility may be:

(i) Put to an alternative use
(ii) Disposed of

Such aspects should also be considered in addition to preferably mutually agreed upon transfer of associated human resources to other divisions.

Similarly, in the event of an insourcing decision, the following situations may emerge and need to be considered:

(i) Existing facilities and human resources may be useful. Therefore, the cost implications pertaining to the decision may not be significant.

(ii) Procurement of additional facilities and hiring of relevant human resources with desired expertise would be necessary. Therefore, significant investment and cost implications arise while implementing the decision.

While outsourcing a certain activity, there might be risk in some cases. For example, in the case of a bicycle maker most of the parts are outsourced. Partial loss of business is observed in a particular segment, that is, smaller cycles used by children. Among other reasons, this is because suppliers or their representatives are able to appeal to some of the potential customers, that is, parents, because parents are normally buying such products for their children. Arguments offered might include the following: as many parts are outsourced in the final product of a brand, parts reliability is similar. Furthermore, even if brand value exists in terms of durability, children may use smaller bicycles for short time only and related doubts may not be so relevant. For a considerable number of customers, this appears convincing. Such aftereffects, among others related to outsourcing, may also be included in specific cases for making a final decision.

5.3 Relationships

If a final decision is in favour of outsourcing, then the relationship between buyer and supplier matters in many situations for attainment of a higher degree of success. In order to provide suitable advice pertaining to outsourcing aspects with inclusion of the supplier relationship, crucial factors related to the problem should be considered. A variety of factors are represented in Figure 5.11.

5.3.1 Price

Price charged by the supplier is a significant factor in most of cases. A lower or competitive price is generally preferred for establishing a long-term relationship if other aspects are reasonably similar. In order to maintain a strategic relationship, the preferred supplier company should be able to control the price of their product despite fluctuations (particularly upwards) in the costs incurred by them in various activities. For example, operational costs have increased at the supplier premises due to any reason such as an increased purchase cost of their raw material. Now in order to maintain a similar profit margin, there might be options such as the following:

(i) Increase the price of the component
(ii) Reduce the overall operational cost

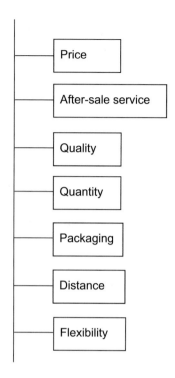

Figure 5.11 Factors influencing relationship

Most of the companies may decide in favour of the first option. However, this may not be welcomed by the buyer. In cases in which it is feasible, the second option should be explored. The possibilities of reducing the overall operational cost despite an increase in a parameter may be analyzed. Depending on company or business analytics, one or more suitable parameter(s) can be altered to achieve the desired objective. A list of parameters might include:

 (i) Ordering cost for raw material
 (ii) Facility setup cost for component
 (iii) Transportation cost of raw material
 (iv) Ordering frequency for raw material
 (v) Production setup frequency for component
 (vi) Related material handling cost
 (vii) Production cost for component
(viii) Inventory carrying cost for raw material
 (ix) Inventory holding cost for component
 (x) Transportation cost for component

For a long-term strategic relationship, the supplier company with favourable parameters might be selected.

5.3.2 *After-sale service*

There are many products that require a certain level of after-sale service, such as:

(i) Water purifier
(ii) Air conditioner
(iii) Refrigerator
(iv) Computer systems

Generally speaking, frequency of service may be low or high. In some cases, regular maintenance is needed and an annual maintenance contract is made between two parties. However, while evaluating the service providers or services given by them, the following aspects should also be considered along with routine performance criteria:

(i) Prompt response
(ii) Excellent service

In many situations, there is a myth such that a prompt response is excellent service. However, this might not be true. Consider an example in which certain equipment is under maintenance and there are two service providers. The experience with both can be narrated as follows:

Service provider #1

After getting a message from the customer company, the response is prompt and a representative visited the location on the same day.

Service provider #2

After getting a message from the customer company, a delayed response came and, finally, the representative could not visit the location on the same day.

Prima facie, it appears that service provider #1 is better. However, the fact might be different. The subsequent experience is narrated as follows:

Service provider #1

Despite visiting on the same day, the problem is not solved. There might be several reasons, such as:

(i) Requisite tools are not available with the person.

(ii) Desired expertise is missing.

(iii) The visiting mechanic and superiors stationed in the office could not determine the real cause of the problem and the associated remedy.

(iv) It appeared that the problem was solved. However, the equipment started malfunctioning again after a few hours.

In this way, the reported problem is sorted out only after five days.

Service provider #2

Although the representative could not visit the location on the same day, as mentioned earlier, the problem is solved fully the next day at the visit. In this way, the reported problem is solved within two days, despite a delayed response along with the visit. Reasons for this relatively better service might include:

(i) After getting the message, the superiors anticipated the real cause of the problem and the associated remedy well. They selected a well-qualified and experienced mechanic accordingly.

(ii) It is ensured that the requisite tools were available with the person.

(iii) The problem is sorted out in one go because of the desired expertise.

(iv) There is better coordination and communication.

Such aspects need to be understood and evaluated appropriately, and accordingly, selection of the suppliers or service providers should be made. This helps a lot in long-term outsourcing relationships.

5.3.3 Quality

Traditionally, quality is considered to be good if an acceptable lot arrives in the buyer organization. However, for a long-term supplier relationship, it is also necessary to analyze the situation further, as shown in Figure 5.12.

At the supplier location, the following situations may emerge:

(i) Acceptable/negligible quality problem

(ii) Unacceptable quality issue

In the case of the negligible or acceptable issue, the supplier company is producing good-quality components. A quality system is built in such a manner that quality defects are negligible and acceptable. This is an ideal scenario because unnecessary cost concerning defects are not incurred at the supplier location and finally the buyer organization is also happy after receiving a good lot continuously.

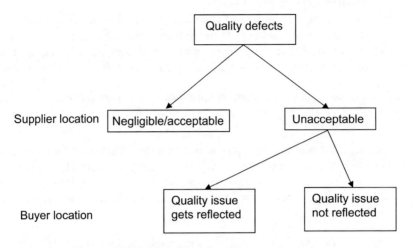

Figure 5.12 Quality issue at supplier/buyer location

When unacceptable quality defects are generated at the supplier location, that is, the number of defects occurring in the production process is greater, then the effects at the buyer location may be of two kinds:

(i) Quality issue gets reflected
(ii) Quality issue not getting reflected

If a quality issue gets reflected at the buyer location, it means that the number of defects getting detected by the buyer is high. In other words, the problem is being passed on to the buyer, affecting the relationship adversely. However, when quality issues are not getting reflected at the buyer location, it means that all the quality defects are detected by the supplier and discarded at their location only. The buyer company is receiving good lots. In such a case, the buyer may feel good about the supplier or supply chain for some time. However, if they are ignorant about a real issue at the supplier location, then the supply may not be efficient because of higher cost of components at the supplier end. It may not be possible to supply at a predetermined price after some time because:

(i) Cost is increased on account of more defects
(ii) Profit margin is either reduced or becoming negligible considering a predetermined price

Because of this, the relationship may not continue for a longer period, and therefore the problem needs to be sorted out with trust and information sharing. In other words, the buyer should not be happy just to receive good lots, but they should also know of real problems at the supplier end if both parties agree to share information for the sake of a long-term relationship.

5.3.4 Quantity

Quantity or demand from the buyer plays a crucial role in the relationship between the buyer and the supplier. Various scenarios need to be understood, as shown in Figure 5.13, on the basis of level of quantity and its fluctuation. Level of quantity and its fluctuation may determine the degree of success in a relationship, and specific scenarios should be analyzed depending on the case, such as:

Scenario I: Low quantity, low fluctuation
Scenario II: Low quantity, high fluctuation
Scenario III: High quantity, high fluctuation
Scenario IV: High quantity, low fluctuation

A guaranteed larger quantity demanded by the buyer helps a lot in planning and execution by the supplier, along with profitability. A large number of resources are devoted to a particular buyer, and a strong long-term relationship gets developed. On the other hand, smaller quantities may not receive much attention from the supplier, and probably both parties may not find it beneficial to pursue a strategic relationship.

Less variation or fluctuation in quantity demanded is usually preferred for the sake of better:

 (i) Production planning/scheduling
 (ii) Machine loading
(iii) Procurement planning for raw material
(iv) Transportation planning for raw material
 (v) Storage of raw material
(vi) Storage of produced items
(vii) Transportation for produced items

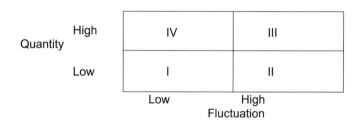

Figure 5.13 Level of quantity/fluctuation

5.3.5 Packaging

The following activities may take place in the pharmaceutical industry in the context of the packaging of medicines:

(i) First, tablets or capsules are packed in strips
(ii) A few strips are put in a certain smaller packet
(iii) A few packets are placed in a large packet
(iv) Finally, the large packet is also packaged/sealed and is made suitable for handling/transportation to various places

In general, packaging plays an important role in material handling and logistics. However, in the supplier–vendor relationship, sometimes issues happen such as:

(i) A standard pack size relates to certain quantities of an item. However, one packet or its multiples may not be equivalent to an optimum purchase lot size for a particular buyer.
(ii) At the supplier location, packaging material and method of packaging is considered to be appropriate. However, the requirement at the buyer location might be different because of reasons including extreme weather conditions such as heavy rains and also very low as well as very high temperatures, depending on the place and time/season.

5.3.6 Distance

In some situations, geographical distance between the supplier and the buyer matters. These may be as follows:

(i) A certain feature in the product is creating a problem at the customer or buyer location. It appears necessary to visit the customer, and therefore the supplier company decides to send their representative. In a case in which the distance between buyer and supplier location is small, it results in shorter time and lower expenditure to settle the issue.
(ii) A buyer company may wish to train vendors concerning the technical and managerial aspects of the business. Hence, their representative has to visit the supplier location. This helps the buyer to see the vendor's operations and facilities as well as to train them on the spot. Close proximity helps in lowering the time, efforts, and incurred costs.
(iii) A supplier caters to the needs of multiple buyers because of certain critical expertise. Since a higher total demand exists than the supplier capacity, it may be needed to prioritize the orders, and also congestion may occur on the shop floor. In such a scenario, a buyer representative might visit the supplier location frequently in order to expedite their

order. It helps a lot if both companies are in a similar industrial area/city or the distance is relatively lower.

5.3.7 Flexibility

In many cases, a buyer company prefers flexibility in supplier operations. This flexibility may relate to:

(i) Quantity
(ii) Lead time
(iii) Design

Required quantity may change, and the supplier should be flexible to accommodate or to allow these changes. Such a change might be upwards as well as downwards; that is, the requirement can increase or decrease. The lead time requirement can also vary from the buyer side, and the supplier should be flexible enough to expedite or delay the operations as per the changed scenario. Design of the component can also change, and the supplier should be capable to produce the suggested changes. Such capabilities in terms of flexibility lead to a strategic partnership/relationship in specific cases.

Additionally, these characteristics might also be needed for a combination of changes such as:

(i) Quantity and lead time
(ii) Quantity and design
(iii) Lead time and design
(iv) Quantity, lead time, and design

In the case of a desired simultaneous change by the buyer in quantity and lead time, the following possibilities might emerge:

(i) Quantity and lead time both increase
(ii) Quantity and lead time both decrease
(iii) Quantity decreases, but desired lead time increases
(iv) Quantity increases, but desired lead time decreases

In the event of an increased quantity, additional challenges arise for the supplier if the buyer somehow also desires a reduction in lead time. With a reduced overall lead time (in comparison with that proposed from the supplier side rationally), if work content increases, then either work cannot be completed or additional resources may be needed if it is possible to arrange. These resources may be in terms of overtime, human resources, availability of additional facility, and space among others. However, this also requires additional cost or expenditure, impacting the profit margin considering a similar price. Otherwise, there may be a need to reconsider the offered price.

Similarly for other combinations of changes including design, the supplier and the buyer may find a mutually agreed upon course of action depending on the associated factors.

5.4 Outsourcing management

Consider the following situations:

(i) An activity was insourced earlier. A decision is made to outsource it, and a suitable supplier or service provider is chosen. After outsourcing for some time, it is decided by the management to insource that again, as shown in Figure 5.14.
(ii) After receiving services or an item, the buyer expresses dissatisfaction. However, the supplier or service provider is unable to understand the evaluation or performance measure, if any.

Such situations, among others, clearly indicate that the outsourcing management needs immediate attention in order to enhance the probability of success while outsourcing. Generally speaking, some of the important aspects concerned with outsourcing management are provided in Figure 5.15.

5.4.1 Specification

Before outsourcing an item, specification needs to be prepared. Major elements of the specification of an item are shown in Figure 5.16.

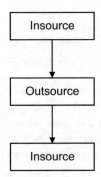

Figure 5.14 In-out-insource

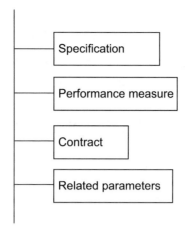

Figure 5.15 Aspects concerned with outsourcing management

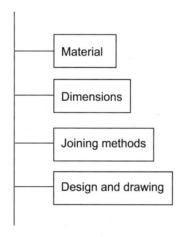

Figure 5.16 Major elements of the item specification

Material should be explicitly specified. For example, in the case of a table, whether it is made of wood or steel as the major material must be specified. Furthermore, it should be indicated whether it is teak wood or mild steel, as there are different types of wood and steel. Precise composition of the specific material may be necessary in certain cases. A wide variety of material may also include plastic, glass, rubber, and ceramic.

After specifying the material, dimensions of different parts of the item must be provided as far as possible. Many of these dimensions may relate to the following:

(i) Length
(ii) Width
(iii) Height
(iv) Thickness
(v) Diameter
(vi) Radius

Wherever necessary, joining methods for various parts might be mentioned. Various joining methods may include:

(i) Welding
(ii) Brazing
(iii) Soldering
(iv) Fasteners
(v) Adhesives

A detailed design and drawing may be provided for certain products. This may also include different views, such as front/top/side views, depending on the need. In addition to precise information, this also helps to visualize how the item will appear.

Although specification is an important aspect concerned with the outsourcing activity, the item should be neither underspecified nor overspecified. If an item is underspecified, that means many details are missing. In such a case, almost every company, whether small, medium, or large, may feel competent to do the job and satisfy the underspecified features. Several companies may respond to the request for a quotation and tender analysis might be difficult.

On the other hand, if each and every minute detail is specified, most companies find it difficult to achieve and satisfy the complete requirement. A very small number of companies might respond to the overspecified features, and competitive offers may not be available. Sometimes an overspecified item may also resemble a particular product from one company, and that may not be desirable.

Degree of specification should be judiciously selected, that is, neither underspecified nor overspecified. Important and critical aspects may be specified, whereas some insignificant and non-critical aspects might be omitted and left to the discretion of a supplier company. An effort should be made to avoid the potential disadvantages of under-/overspecification .

5.4.2 Performance measure

While outsourcing an activity, it is also necessary to think about suitable performance measures. Some of these may pertain to:

(i) Timely delivery
(ii) Quality measures

(iii) Overall procurement cost
(iv) After-sale service
 (v) Equipment uptime
(vi) Frequency of equipment failure
(vii) Cleanliness

Some measures are easier to quantify. However, qualitative judgement may be allowed in some issues, such as cleanliness if a housekeeping job is out-sourced. Wherever possible, a suitable measure should be developed and it should be explicitly understood by both parties, that is, buyer and supplier or service provider. In order to avoid any ill feeling about the performance evaluation, where possible, an effort can be made to introduce transparency in issues such as:

 (i) Explicit measure and its rationale
(ii) Method of collecting data
(iii) Process of analyzing information
(iv) Arriving at the final measure
 (v) Comparison of suppliers/service providers
(vi) Other associated unique aspect

5.4.3 Contract

A contract between two parties should be reasonably balanced. It cannot go excessively in favour of one party, that is, either buyer or supplier. For instance, whatever cost or expenditure is incurred by the supplier or service provider, a guaranteed profit margin is allowed over it. Despite the advantage of such a contract, a service provider in certain cases may not make efforts to reduce or control their costs or expenditure as time passes. It may be necessary to examine whether such a contract goes excessively in favour of the service provider in specific cases.

On the other hand, if price is not revised despite an increase in input item cost, this goes in favour of the buyer. For example, in the case of galvanized iron pipe, zinc coating is done on the pipe for making it corrosion-resistant. Suppliers of such pipe are affected if price is not revised despite an increase in zinc prices. A price escalation clause is helpful in such a case in which the price of the pipe can vary without any formal buyer approval, depending on the increase in zinc price. Standard information in this regard may either be available or can be developed. For instance, in the case of a specific pipe of a certain diameter and thickness, weight of the zinc per metre of pipe can be obtained after getting information such as:

 (i) Perimeter of the pipe
(ii) Thickness of the zinc coating

(iii) Volume of the zinc per metre length of pipe
(iv) Density of zinc

Once the weight of zinc per metre length of pipe is known, the effect on price can easily be determined per metre length of pipe.

5.4.4 Related parameters

While selecting the supplier company for the short/medium/long term, related parameters might play a significant role. Consider the following situations:

(i) The normal requirement of the buyer is small periodically; however, a larger requirement should be satisfied immediately whenever it is needed. Now the supplier may be expected to produce in bigger lot sizes and carry the inventory. Under such a scenario, inventory carrying cost becomes a significant parameter. If it is lower for a particular supplier, it becomes an added advantage.

(ii) The buyer follows just-in-time principles, and requirement is almost uniform. The expectation from the supplier is production of smaller quantities with higher frequency. Under such a scenario, facility setup cost becomes a significant parameter. If it is lower for a particular supplier, it becomes an added advantage.

(iii) While outsourcing catering services, food quality and shelf life might be issues in a certain case. However, there might be a linkage with the packaging method and packaging materials also. Such parameters or factors need a thorough study and analysis for suggesting an appropriate course of action, including remedial measures. Additionally, in the context of newly introduced regulations, there may be an urgent requirement for replacing the packaging material in order to make it environmentally friendly.

For a wide variety of situations, certain related parameters might be the focus of attention while outsourcing. These parameters/factors may include:

  (i) Facility setup cost
 (ii) Inventory holding cost
(iii) Stock out cost
(iv) Cycle time
 (v) Production rate
(vi) Smooth supply of raw material
(vii) Procurement cost of raw material
(viii) Facility layout
(ix) Material handling
 (x) Quality
(xi) Flexibility

(xii) Price
(xiii) After-sale service
(xiv) Packaging
 (xv) Shelf life
(xvi) Lead time

Certain important aspects pertaining to outsourcing management have been mentioned, including the specification, performance measure, contract balance, and related parameters. Depending on the analysis of a particular assignment, a parameter or a suitable set of parameters should be identified and corresponding advice should be forwarded for the related outsourcing issues that have arisen in the business.

Exercises

1 Explain how the following terms have a more or less similar meaning:

   (i) Purchase or buy
   (ii) Externalizing/externalize
   (iii) Outsourcing/outsource

2 Discuss how the following terms have a more or less similar meaning:

   (i) Make or produce
   (ii) Internalizing/internalize
   (iii) Insourcing/insource

3 Before outsourcing any activity, for example, manufacturing of a component, elaborate why the types of factors to be considered broadly are as follows:

   (i) Cost factors
   (ii) Non-cost factors

4 Describe how the cost factors should be viewed from these two sides:

   (i) Associated cost while insourcing
   (ii) Associated cost while outsourcing

5 Explain the following factors for cost while insourcing:

   (i) Raw material purchase cost
   (ii) Raw material transportation cost
   (iii) Manufacturing cost
   (iv) Material handling cost

6 Provide a detailed comment on the following.
   If it is intended to manufacture a component within the house, then the following two situations emerge:

(i) Fixed assets/machinery may not be available. In a normal case, if a certain machine is required to produce a component, then it may be procured and installed. However, in cases in which a machine or a set of workstations needs a lot of space, then the availability of area might be a significant problem because of congestion.

(ii) Machinery is available in the plant and therefore might be utilized to produce the intended component in addition to the existing jobs being processed currently on that machine.

7 Differentiate between major and minor setups in the tabular form.
8 Provide a detailed comment on the following.
   In addition to the manufacturing cost, material handling within the plant should also be studied. Material handling cost specifically pertaining to the component insourced depends on:

   (i) Material flow and movement
   (ii) Equipment used for handling
   (iii) Source of power for the material handling equipment
   (iv) Quantity to be handled

9 Explain the following factors for cost while outsourcing:

   (i) Component purchase cost
   (ii) Component transportation cost
   (iii) Storage/inventory cost
   (iv) Supplier selection

10 Provide a detailed discussion of the following activities:

   (i) Finalize the specification for the component along with other terms and conditions
   (ii) Invite the quotation/notice inviting tender
   (iii) Tender evaluation
   (iv) Supplier selection
   (v) Periodic supplier evaluation and review
   (vi) Coordination efforts

11 Discuss a comparison of associated cost while:

   (i) Insourcing
   (ii) Outsourcing

12 Describe how a final decision whether to outsource is made.
13 A steel tube manufacturing company produces tube/pipe in a variety of:

   (i) Diameters
   (ii) Thicknesses
   (iii) Lengths

The immediate input item is cold rolled coil for certain products. Coils are slit into a suitable width, and the appropriate width of the coil is formed into pipe or tube and finally welded and cut to a suitable length. The mentioned input item, that is, those coils, can be procured from outside. However, there is considerable distance between the major supplier company and the buyer, that is, the steel tube manufacturing company. Because of this, the transportation cost is higher. Depending on the thickness of the final product, that is, steel tube, a wide variety of thicknesses of the coil is needed. Analyze the following two options this company has:

(a) Procure a wide variety of thicknesses of coil and directly take the coil to the tube mill as an input item.
(b) Procure very few thicknesses of coil and introduce an intermediate operation for reducing the thickness to the precise need of steel tube.

14 The L.P.G. cylinder is fabricated after welding two halves. In the upper half, a forged steel part called a bung is welded, after creating a circular hole on top of the upper half and degreasing this. This part has internal threads for fitting of the brass valve later at the final stage. By using a submerged arc along with a copper-coated mild steel electrode, bung welding is done after fitting it in the hole punched on the upper half.

Provide a suitable argument in favour of outsourcing this part.

15 Manufacturing of a part that is traditionally outsourced by the L.P.G. cylinder manufacturing company is mentioned in the previous exercise. This part has internal threads, and at the end of production processes, a brass valve with external threads is tightened over the mentioned part on the top portion of the cylinder.

The utility of the brass valve lies in its ability to allow the exit of gas and also stoppage with the help of a regulator fitted on the valve during actual use. Provide a suitable argument in favour of outsourcing the production of this valve.

16 Comment on the risk involved in outsourcing a certain activity.

17 If a final decision is in favour of outsourcing, then the relationship between buyer and supplier matters in many situations for attainment of a higher degree of success. With the inclusion of the supplier relationship, discuss factors such as:

(i) Price
(ii) After-sale service
(iii) Quality
(iv) Quantity
(v) Packaging
(vi) Distance
(vii) Flexibility

18 For a long-term strategic relationship, the supplier company with favourable parameters might be selected. In this context, elaborate the following parameters:

    (i) Ordering cost for raw material
    (ii) Facility setup cost for component
    (iii) Transportation cost of raw material
    (iv) Ordering frequency for raw material
    (v) Production setup frequency for component
    (vi) Related material handling cost
    (vii) Production cost for component
    (viii) Inventory carrying cost for raw material
    (ix) Inventory holding cost for component
    (x) Transportation cost for component

19 Generally speaking, frequency of service may be low or high. In some cases, regular maintenance is needed and an annual maintenance contract is made between two parties. However, while evaluating the service providers or services given by them, the following aspects should also be considered along with routine performance criteria:

    (i) Prompt response
    (ii) Excellent service

Differentiate between prompt service and excellent service with the use of a suitable example.

20 Traditionally, quality is considered to be good if an acceptable lot arrives in the buyer organization. However, for a long-term supplier relationship, it is also necessary to further analyze the situation. Describe in detail the quality issue at the supplier/buyer location as follows:

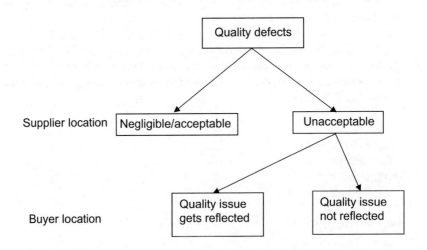

21 Elaborate how less variation or fluctuation in quantity demanded is usually preferred for the sake of better:

   (i) Production planning/scheduling
   (ii) Machine loading
   (iii) Procurement planning for raw material
   (iv) Transportation planning for raw material
   (v) Storage of raw material
   (vi) Storage of produced item
   (vii) Transportation for produced item

22 In general, packaging plays an important role in material handling and logistics. However, in the supplier–vendor relationship, comment on the following issues that might happen:

   (i) A standard pack size relates to certain quantities of an item. However, one packet or its multiples may not be equivalent to an optimum purchase lot size for a particular buyer.
   (ii) At the supplier location, packaging material and method of packaging are considered to be appropriate. However, the requirement at the buyer location might be different because of reasons including extreme weather conditions, such as heavy rains, and also very low as well as very high temperatures depending on the place and time/season.

23 Under what situations does geographical distance between supplier and buyer matter?

24 In many cases, a buyer company prefers flexibility in supplier operations. Discuss how this flexibility may relate to:

   (i) Quantity
   (ii) Lead time
   (iii) Design

25 Explain the combination of changes such as:

   (i) Quantity and lead time
   (ii) Quantity and design
   (iii) Lead time and design
   (iv) Quantity, lead time, and design

26 In the case of the desired simultaneous change by the buyer in quantity and lead time, comment on the following possibilities that might emerge:

   (i) Quantity and lead time both increase
   (ii) Quantity and lead time both decrease
   (iii) Quantity decreases, but desired lead time increases
   (iv) Quantity increases, but desired lead time decreases

27 Describe what you understand by outsourcing management in the context of the following situations:

   (i) An activity was insourced earlier. A decision is made to outsource it, and a suitable supplier or service provider is chosen. After outsourcing it for some time, it is decided by the management to insource that again.
   (ii) After receiving services or an item, the buyer expresses dissatisfaction. However, the supplier or service provider is unable to understand the evaluation or performance measure, if any.

28 Explain the important aspects concerned with outsourcing management, such as:

   (i) Specification
   (ii) Performance measure
   (iii) Contract
   (iv) Related parameters

29 In order to avoid any ill feeling about the performance evaluation, elaborate how an effort can be made to introduce transparency in issues such as:

   (i) Explicit measure and its rationale
   (ii) Method of collecting data
   (iii) Process of analyzing information
   (iv) Arriving at the final measure
   (v) Comparison of suppliers/service providers

30 A contract should not go excessively in favour of one party, that is, either buyer or supplier. How can a contract between two parties be reasonably balanced?

31 While selecting the supplier company for the short/medium/long term, related parameters might play a significant role. For a wide variety of situations with a focus of attention while outsourcing, discuss the following related parameters/factors:

   (i) Facility setup cost
   (ii) Inventory holding cost
   (iii) Stock out cost
   (iv) Cycle time
   (v) Production rate
   (vi) Smooth supply of raw material
   (vii) Procurement cost of raw material
   (viii) Facility layout
   (ix) Material handling
   (x) Quality
   (xi) Flexibility

(xii) Price
(xiii) After-sale service
(xiv) Packaging
 (xv) Shelf life
(xvi) Lead time

32 In order to outsource production of an item, certain specifications need to be created. Describe what happens when an item is:

(i) Underspecified
(ii) Overspecified

33 Quantity or demand from the buyer plays a crucial role in the relationship between buyer and supplier. Explain various scenarios that need to be understood as illustrated on the basis of level of quantity and its fluctuation:

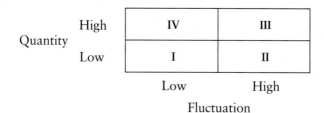

34 While outsourcing an activity, it is also necessary to think about suitable performance measures. Discuss how some of these may pertain to:

  (i) Timely delivery
 (ii) Quality measure
(iii) Overall procurement cost
(iv) After-sale service
  (v) Equipment uptime
 (vi) Frequency of equipment failure
(vii) Cleanliness

35 In the case of galvanized iron pipe, zinc coating is done on the pipe for making it corrosion-resistant. Suppliers of such pipe are affected if the price is not revised to reflect increases in zinc prices. A price escalation clause is helpful in such cases in which price of the pipe can vary without any formal buyer approval depending on the increase in zinc prices. Standard information in this regard may either be available or be developed. For instance, in the case of a specific pipe of a certain diameter and thickness, weight of the zinc per metre of pipe can be obtained after getting information such as:

(i) Perimeter of the pipe
(ii) Thickness of the zinc coating

(iii) Volume of the zinc per metre length of pipe

(iv) Density of zinc

Elaborate how the effect on price can easily be determined per metre length of pipe with the use of such information.

36 While outsourcing catering services, food quality and shelf life might be issues in certain cases. However, there might also be a certain linkage with the packaging method and packaging materials. Comment on such a linkage.

37 A buyer follows just-in-time principles and requirement is almost uniform. The expectation from the supplier is production of smaller quantities with higher frequency. Under such a scenario, what becomes a significant parameter? And when does it become an added advantage?

38 The normal requirement of the buyer is small; periodically, however, a larger requirement should be satisfied immediately whenever it is needed. Under such a scenario, what becomes a significant parameter? And when does it become an added advantage?

6

CONSULTANCY VISION

The vision for consultancy may include a futuristic approach along with the influence of various factors. Such a futuristic approach naturally includes the role of technology. In order to improve efficiency or productivity, among other objectives, an influence of infrastructure on various factors and choices is also specifically introduced in this concluding chapter.

6.1 Futuristic approach

A closer examination of potential happenings in the form, nature, and behaviour of available resources helps in creating an idea for industrial consultancy in the future, both distant and not so distant. Some of the available resources are shown in Figure 6.1.

Analysis pertaining to location can be made depending on the possibility of the location changing its form, for example, from rural to urban, in a reasonable period. From the environment point of view also, it is of some help to foresee matters related to:

 (i) Rain
 (ii) Temperature
(iii) Humidity
(iv) Storm
 (v) Air quality
(vi) Soil

For instance, soil analysis can provide certain important details pertaining to the foundation of a single floor/multiple floors. Along with advancements including a better-informed approach, the location and area available for layout can be analyzed simultaneously or iteratively.

For example, recall that a 'U' type of layout may be used for many products. Layout of the facilities is arranged in the location/area available. The organization may come across two situations, as shown in Figure 6.2, where a layout is represented by 'U' in the available area that may be smaller or larger relatively.

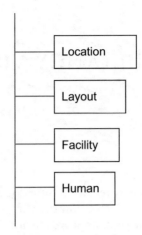

Figure 6.1 Resources

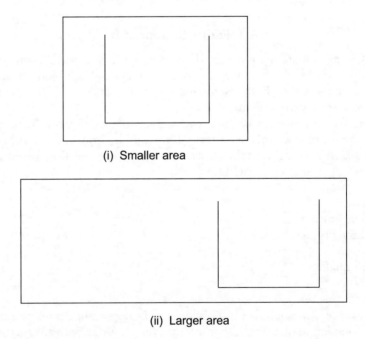

Figure 6.2 Smaller/larger area

Depending on the location, either a smaller or larger area might be available for installing the facilities in a 'U' type of layout, for example. In the first situation, the area is just enough to be covered by the layout, along with only essential space for additional activities such as inbound and outbound logistics. In such a case, traditionally, future expansion in terms of facilities/ layout might appear difficult. However, in the second case, enough space is available for expansion considering the potential demand increase. Having a smaller or larger area might depend on the following aspects:

(i) Ownership of land for the last many years
(ii) Price of the land in the case of a recent purchase
(iii) Rural/urban location
(iv) Availability constraint for the land
(v) Negligible chance for a demand increase for a similar product

Yet in the context of a futuristic approach, there is a considerable possibility of such divisions, that is, smaller/larger area, not being treated as a hindrance/advantage.

Conventionally machines, particularly heavy machines, are preferred on the ground floor only. However, it might be possible to create a similar layout including heavy machines on the floors above the ground floor. In the case of a very high price of the land, the division of smaller/larger area may not be so relevant. Still there would be a trade-off concerning the land price and the aspects such as:

(i) Foundation and structural complexity
(ii) Logistical issues related to the installation of heavy machines on the first floor and above
(iii) Inbound logistics (for raw material/input items) in the context of the first floor and above
(iv) Outbound logistics (for output items) in the context of the first floor and above

Furthermore, a sincere effort towards making machines/handling equipment lighter by innovators/entrepreneurs/related industry would go a long way, thus providing altogether a new business opportunity. A representation of a similar layout on the first floor and above is available in Figure 6.3. With such an approach, keeping a portion of a larger area idle for a longer period may not be required. And as per the requirement, a similar layout can be installed on the first floor and above while solving the potential problems with the help of innovative development in this field.

Thus, there is a huge possibility of a change in approach in the context of future expansion. Traditionally, location or available area is expected to be appropriate for a certain layout. However, the reverse can also become a reality in the distant future, when layout can also adjust with location or available area. This leads to opportunities for other companies/businesses concerning aspects such as design, installation, operation, and maintenance of suitable:

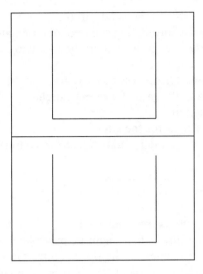

Figure 6.3 Representation of a similar layout on more than one floor

(i) Lifts
(ii) Cranes
(iii) Elevators
(iv) Equipment

The horizon of industrial consultancy also widens with the inclusion of the discussed arena and expertise at a strategic as well as an operational level. Figure 6.4 shows a switch from 'location should be compatible with the layout' to 'layout can also be compatible with the location or area available'.

In the context of facilities also, it is possible to have certain design changes by the OEMs so that these become compatible with the layout or area available. However, such design changes depend on:

(i) Nature of the product being processed
(ii) Mechanism of the machine
(iii) Reliability aspects concerning the facility
(iv) Degree of modularization
(v) Obsolescence

For example, in rubber tube production, one process is extrusion related to the input item. The facility associated with this process traditionally is horizontal, that is, it occupies more space horizontally than vertically. However, there is considerable scope to make this facility as vertical by the OEM, that is, it would

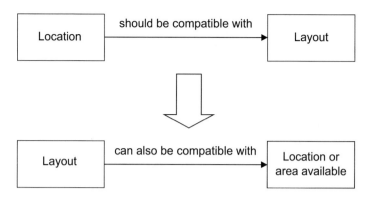

Figure 6.4 Switching to an alternative approach

occupy less space horizontally. In the case of availability of a smaller area and corresponding layout, such a transformed facility would be more appropriate with certain design changes and input item flow process modification.

However, while transforming any facility, generally care should be taken in terms of:

(i) Flow of material during the process
(ii) Effects on tooling and tool life
(iii) Effects on installation
(iv) Operational convenience
(v) Maintenance convenience
(vi) Foundation requirements
(vii) Rigidity
(viii) Substitution of material for the machine parts

Thus, there is huge possibility in the context of facility. Figure 6.5 shows a switch from 'layout or area should be compatible with the facility' to 'facility can also be made compatible with layout or area available'.

In the context of human resources, often an interaction of persons with facilities is closely observed to provide a recommendation for improvement. Recall the following scenario.

In a pharmaceutical company, a portion of the production line is devoted to packaging the tablets among other things. Persons' activities need to be synchronized with the packaging activities.

Each strip consists of a few tablets. A few strips are then put in a packet. A few packets are put in a carton, and then a few cartons are placed on a pallet. Additionally, the packaging speed can be observed, and it is possible to determine the outcome per unit time.

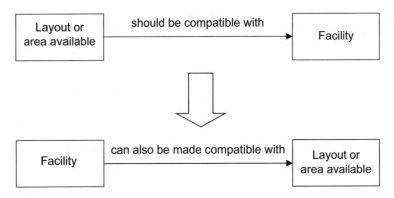

Figure 6.5 Switching to a modified approach

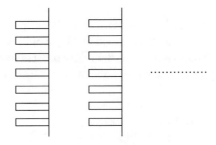

Figure 6.6 Representation of existing line alignment

If the number of persons is fewer, palletizing may get delayed. On the other hand, if the number of persons is greater, idle time of the person can be observed. Accordingly, a suitable number of persons can be proposed. Additionally, the overall design/layout of the packaging lines may be studied. For example, all the lines are aligned on one side, as shown in Figure 6.6.

Traditionally, one person is deputed at the end of each line at the interface of cartons and pallets, among others. It is observed that the mentioned one person can handle two lines if it is possible to change the alignment, as shown in Figure 6.7.

In this way, it is possible to reduce the number of persons to almost half for this specific activity. This may be possible after a thorough study of the interaction of human resources and the production/packaging line. As mentioned earlier, certain recommendations in general can be provided in the context of human resources after closely observing the interaction of persons with facilities.

However, with advancements including robotics, human resources may get replaced by robots for many industrial activities; therefore, the concept

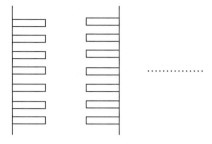

Figure 6.7 Representation of potential line alignment

of speed and the interaction of a robot with other facilities and also human resources would require a new way of looking at the scenario. After a detailed study of the futuristic specific industrial environment, certain questions would need to be answered such as:

(i) How many robots would be optimal?
(ii) Would a robot work alone in a particular area or along with human resources?
(iii) How would division of work take place among human resources and robots?
(iv) What will be the economic impact?

6.2 Role of technology

As technology, including robotics, plays a significant role in industries including SMEs, this should also be included in the visionary approach. Its role needs to be understood for production operations as well as service operations. For production operations, the trend is obviously towards automation and robotics; however, a judicious blend of human resources and robots would depend on aspects such as:

(i) Country
(ii) Locality
(iii) Culture
(iv) Investment scenario
(v) Return on investment
(vi) Payback period

In the context of industries in general and SMEs in particular, level of investment, return on investment, and payback period are crucial factors. Therefore, in many cases, there may not be 100% automation and robot deployment, but partial deployment might be more the appropriate technology and approach. Generally speaking, it might be appropriate technology instead of 'high tech' if similar quality output (or appropriate quality output for a specific customer segment) is available economically.

As mentioned before, a 'U' type of layout may be used for many products. Layout of the facilities is arranged in the location/area available. Traditionally, a focus may be on the movement of material and persons, as shown in Figure 6.8.

Additionally, provision or care should be taken for robot movement in the layout, as shown in Figure 6.9.

Collaboration of human resources with robot resources has to be additionally planned and executed successfully in many cases. A switch to additional movement in the context of a futuristic vision is represented by Figure 6.10. This also requires a certain implication for space. For instance, a joint maintenance operation of a heavy machine (considering both an experienced worker and a robot together) needs enough space for their standing as well as movement adjacent to the machine on all sides (or relevant side) for:

(i) Removal of the spare part
(ii) Replacing the spare part

While adopting technology, including robotics, two types of situations may be faced:

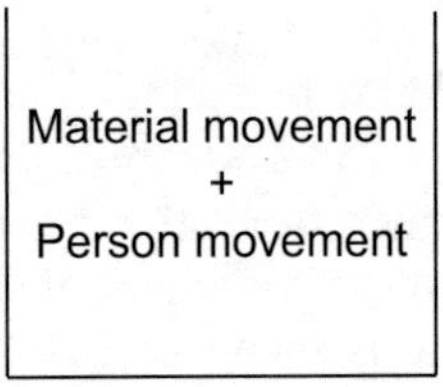

Material movement
+
Person movement

Figure 6.8 Traditional consideration

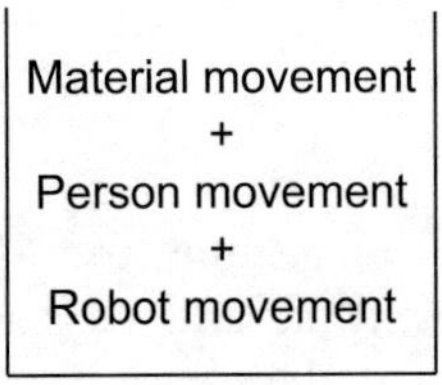

Material movement
+
Person movement
+
Robot movement

Figure 6.9 Potential consideration

170

Figure 6.10 Switching to additional movement

(i) Layout and other details are to be evolved from scratch for a new organization. Therefore, the interaction of the facility, human resources, and robots might be visualized, and accordingly layout including suitable space between facilities can be provided.

(ii) For an older, established organization, the processes already exist and now an attempt is being made to adopt new technology. Under such a scenario, the transitional phase continues for a considerable number of years, and also there might be switching back on account of one or more issues. For instance, an example of maintenance operation of a heavy machine was discussed earlier. The robot alone may recognize the spare part and replace it with certain effort. However, in order to avoid multiple attempts and potential failure during the transitional phase, the discussed collaboration of human resources and robots might be unavoidable. For ease in operations, it is of considerable help if a provision has been made for appropriate space for movement of:

(a) Material
(b) Person
(c) Robot

In many situations, various types of technologies and processes may coexist because of different constraints and limitations such as:

(i) Different places in the plant where processes are carried out
(ii) Different quality requirements
(iii) Limitations on availability of appropriate equipment at all places simultaneously

Recall the case of an L.P.G. cylinder manufacturing company:
This company purchased a larger area for expansion purposes. The available larger area also has enough open space. Additionally, this can be utilized for certain operations on used cylinders. As shown in Figure 6.11, the consumer company, that is, the oil company, can send the used cylinders periodically to the manufacturing company for minor/major repair.

171

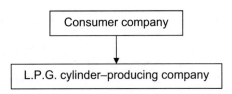

Figure 6.11 Receiving used cylinders for repair

The first operation is degassing the used cylinders, as those might carry a small amount of gas. It is preferred to do this operation in an open space as far as possible. This is also an important locational advantage for the manufacturing company. Depending on minor/major repair, a certain sequence of operations is to be carried out after degassing. In a case in which only a small dent is visible on the cylinder body, this can be rectified. Similarly, if only the paint has worn out, surface finishing such as painting can be done. With these issues, surface finishing and testing such as leakage testing would be enough.

In the context of forward logistics for new cylinders, mechanized equipment with a conveyor system and other modern technologies can be utilized for enhanced quality level requirements related to operations such as painting. However, because of limitations in availability of such a system for the reverse logistics scenario concerning repair of used cylinders, an alternative process may be adopted at another place subject to meeting the desired quality levels. In such a situation, a low-cost arrangement may also be developed. A representation of this arrangement is shown in Figure 6.12.

After various repair processes on the used cylinders, they need to be painted. A cylinder can hang on the developed structure with the help of a hook. In order to avoid friction, rollers can be used, and it is possible to move the cylinder manually after painting is done. It can reciprocate towards the protruding portion of the structure, which is at a certain angle from the horizontal plane so that the cylinder can be lowered at a suitable height on the structure with a certain speed before halting. Finally, the painted cylinder is available at the lowest height on the structure and can be downloaded manually (or with a semi-automated process if it is desirable). Because of the energy in the moving cylinder, it is better to lift the last portion of the structure (adjacent to the lowest-height portion) at a certain angle so that the cylinder may not fall after coming to the lowest-height portion. In the case of the remaining speed, it may climb to that last portion up to some distance and can come back to the lowest-height portion for final downloading.

In addition to production operations, a significant role of technology exists in the context of service operations.

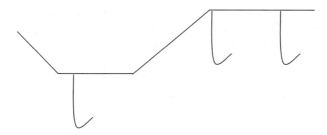

Figure 6.12 A low-cost arrangement for painting the used cylinder

In the context of warehousing services, activities can be automated to a large extent. In the case of a need, a voice-based response might be created for searching/selecting the items in the warehouse. RFID and the associated advancements help a lot in modernizing warehouse activities along with the cost-benefit analysis. Along with systems concerning real-time geographical location, the truck drivers may also switch to computer-aided support while being behind the wheel. However, necessary skills need to be developed along with the desired training and orientation. Such skills may include:

(i) Maintenance of the desired temperature for a certain category of items
(ii) Time management related to arrival at the intended destination
(iii) Coordination with other support services such as those related to the loading and unloading of items

Additionally, wherever possible and efficient, such as inside the warehouse, electric vehicles may be made operational along with necessary facilities at appropriate places. Therefore, the role of technology may be suitably studied before providing a recommendation, depending on the type of industry and associated activities. This should also happen after establishing the link with performance measures among other goals of the organization and society as a whole.

6.3 Infrastructure influence

Overall infrastructure available influences the working of a particular organization as well as providing certain recommendations as an outcome of a consultancy assignment. In cases in which a favourable infrastructure is available at a particular geographic location, it helps a lot in the following:

(i) Installation, operation, and maintenance of appropriate facilities and technology

(ii) Effective utilization of layout horizontally as well as vertically
(iii) Easy approachability by the concerned parties such as suppliers, service providers, and also customer representatives

As shown in Figure 6.13, choice of location, layout, facilities and technology, and people are affected directly or indirectly by the availability of infrastructure or potential infrastructure.

6.3.1 Location

Infrastructure may be favourable from an industry point of view, such as good roads, connectivity, and cold storage as per the case. Connectivity may be in terms of rail, road, air, and water depending on the case. Good infrastructure in general can lead to a favourable choice.

6.3.2 Layout

Link of layout with location has been discussed earlier, along with inter-dependencies. If good infrastructure is available, it might be convenient to arrange for equipment and associated arrangement for installation and maintenance of facilities on more than one floor in the layout. In this way, effective utilization of layout happens vertically in addition to horizontally.

6.3.3 Facilities and technology

Facilities are built on certain principles and characteristic features including the technology aspects. As mentioned earlier, there is a link between layout

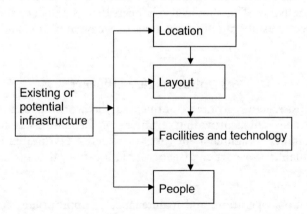

Figure 6.13 Influence of infrastructure

and facilities/technology. For technology development and adoption, the following types of situations may emerge:

(i) The organization itself develops the technology
(ii) The suppliers themselves develop the technology along with a negligible role of the buyer organization
(iii) Both the organization and its supplier collaborate in developing the technology and related aspects

The technology may relate to both product as well as process/facility. In a case in which collaboration with the supplier is desirable, good existing or potential infrastructure contributes positively towards greater, more efficient, and more effective collaboration.

6.3.4 People

Infrastructure may be good from an industry point of view, that is, a logistical point of view. However, it may not be so from the people perspective. People in general and employees of an organization, in particular, are more affected by the infrastructure in terms of good:

(i) Hospital/medical facilities
(ii) Educational institutes
(iii) Housing

In the absence of such types of facilities, it might be difficult to retain employees. In order to operate and maintain a modernized factory, directly or indirectly, good-quality people are needed, including their involvement in design and innovative activities every now and then, in order to make the organization competitive.

Because of considerable infrastructure influence, there is significant potential for partnership or collaboration with developers of various facilities such as housing. In addition to good connectivity from a logistical point of view, good and affordable housing can be developed as per the need or in anticipation as the case may be. A very well-considered plan helps in development at a low cost, and that is beneficial to all concerned, such as industry, developers, employees, and people in general. There is also scope for application of supply chain concepts in project management such as provision for housing.

Timely availability of housing is critical in some cases. Various activities in this regard include arrangement of different agencies to do the construction work, electrical work, and finishing, after procurement of a suitable area of land in the locality. These activities consume considerable time. There are several goals, such as project cost, availability, offered price for the customers, and lead time. In order to reduce the lead time regarding provision for housing, the collaborative plan after inclusion of multiple objectives should consider the following aspects:

  (i) Whether procurement of land happens after getting the final booking
 (ii) Whether procurement of land happens well in advance in anticipation
(iii) Whether project or construction activity should begin after the potential building or house gets booked
(iv) Whether the construction or project work should begin in anticipation of demands

6.4 Channel design

Conventionally, the channel related to a particular business/industry might be confined to the aspects shown in Figure 6.14.

Depending on the industry, input item suppliers might have their premises close to the buyer organization or far away from it. Procurement of raw materials/input items and production of final product are essential components of a manufacturing organization. However, in certain cases, design of the product also is a significant activity and provides important information for procurement and production functions. As logistics traditionally refers to transportation and warehousing, these activities also come under the channel design. With the customer interface, the marketing function along

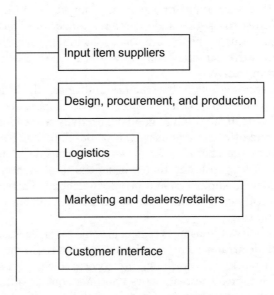

Figure 6.14 Aspects related to the conventional channel

with the retailer/dealer network provides a lot of important information for the whole chain, including customer demands.

Depending on the customer demand among other details, the whole supply chain design incorporates the following issues among others:

(i) How many suppliers are suitable: a few, many, or one?
(ii) Linking design according to customer orders and also procurement of input items and production of final product as per the demand/design
(iii) Number of warehouses and transportation planning
(iv) Dealer network, that is, how many dealers are suitable?
(v) Customer satisfaction approaches

As a promising approach towards channel design, additional attention, as represented in Figure 6.15, should be made to have a holistic view with respect to:

(i) Linking location with layout
(ii) Linking layout with facility and technology
(iii) Appropriate combination of automation and human resources
(iv) Enabling infrastructure

For the enabling infrastructure, collaboration may happen well in advance either at a government level, a corporate level, or both, depending on the scenario.

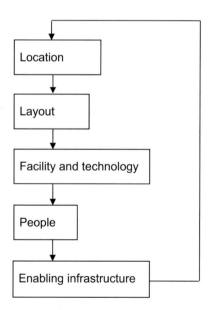

Figure 6.15 Additional attention for a holistic view

For instance, if roads are available on both sides of the layout, there is a possibility of separate gates for entry and exit depending on the material flow lines of the layout among other factors. As was mentioned earlier, facility and technology may correspond to the layout which, in turn, may correspond to the location or area available for the organization. Therefore, such a perfect linking in addition to a conventional channel design is highly useful for overall satisfaction of all concerned such as:

(i) Government
(ii) Industry
(iii) Channel partners
(iv) Firms in collaboration/cooperation
(v) Employees
(vi) Society

In addition to roads and connectivity concerning overall infrastructure, housing needs to be addressed with prediction of demands. With enabling infrastructure, the logistical benefits among others can go to a whole cluster of companies. Benefits of the economies of scale concerning transportation can be achieved by cooperation among different companies in the locality or industrial area, depending on their requirement of input items and sales of their finished products among other factors.

This book has described some key aspects of industrial consultancy: industrial location, productivity, and lead time, along with an analysis on practical outsourcing provided for the benefit of readers. Finally, a futuristic approach has been proposed to augment the vision of consultancy, and I hope this helps with these aims and pursuits.

Exercises

1 A closer examination of potential happenings in the form, nature, and behaviour of available resources helps in creating an idea for industrial consultancy in the future. In this context, explain some of the available resources such as:

   (i) Location
   (ii) Layout
   (iii) Facility
   (iv) Human

2 Discuss how, from the environmental point of view, it is of some help to foresee matters related to:

   (i) Rain
   (ii) Temperature
   (iii) Humidity

(iv) Storms

(v) Air quality

(vi) Soil

3 Explain how possession of smaller or larger area might depend on the following aspects:

(i) Ownership of land for the last many years

(ii) Price of the land in the case of a recent purchase

(iii) Rural/urban location

(iv) Availability constraint for the land

(v) Negligible chance for demand increase for a similar product

4 A 'U' type of layout may be used for many products. Layout of the facilities is arranged in the location/area available. The organization may come across two situations in which a layout exists in the available area that may be smaller or larger relatively.

Elaborate, in terms of future expansion, what happens traditionally when such a layout is arranged in a smaller area as follows:

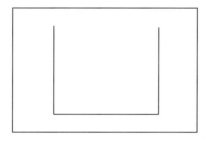

Also elaborate, in terms of future expansion, what happens when such a layout is arranged in a larger area as follows:

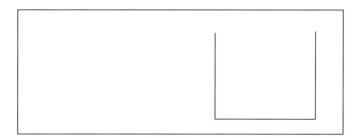

5 When an area is just large enough to be covered by the layout, traditionally future expansion in terms of facilities/layout might appear difficult. Yet in the context of a futuristic approach, there is a considerable possibility of such divisions, that is, smaller/larger area, not being treated as

179

a hindrance/advantage. In a case in which a smaller area exists within an industrial organization and there is a need for expansion, elaborate the potential for a similar layout on more than one floor as follows:

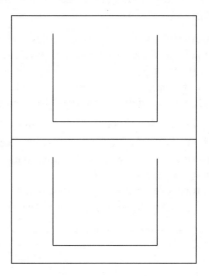

6 Depending on the location, a smaller or larger area is available within the existing organization. Traditionally, a location or available area is expected to be appropriate for a certain layout. However, the reverse can also become a reality in the distant future when layout can adjust with location or available area. Thus, there is a huge possibility in change of approach in the context of future expansion. In the context of a futuristic approach for the consultancy vision, describe in detail the potential for switching to an alternative approach as follows:

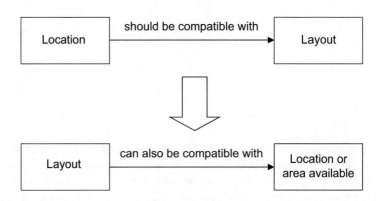

7 It is possible to have certain design changes by the OEMs so that facilities become compatible with the layout or area available. Explain how such design changes depend on:

(i) Nature of the product being processed
(ii) Mechanism of the machine
(iii) Reliability aspects concerning the facility
(iv) Degree of modularization
(vi) Obsolescence

8 While transforming any facility, discuss how care should be taken in terms of:

(i) Flow of material during the process
(ii) Effects on tooling and tool life
(iii) Effects on installation
(iv) Operational convenience
(v) Maintenance convenience
(vi) Foundation requirements
(vii) Rigidity
(viii) Substitution of material for the machine parts

9 Describe how a judicious blend of human resources and robots would depend on aspects such as:

(i) Country
(ii) Locality
(iii) Culture
(iv) Investment scenario
(v) Return on investment
(vi) Payback period

10 In the context of a futuristic approach for the consultancy vision, discuss in detail the potential for switching to a modified approach as follows:

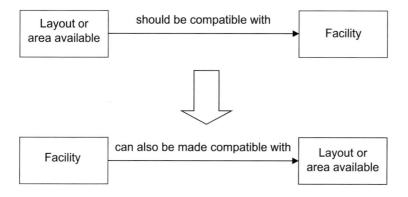

11 After a detailed study of the futuristic, specific industrial environment, elaborate why certain questions would need to be answered such as:

(i) How many robots would be optimal?
(ii) Would the robot be alone in a particular area or with human resources?
(iii) How would division of work take place among human resources and robots?
(iv) What will be the economic impact?

12 Describe the scope for switching to additional movement as follows:

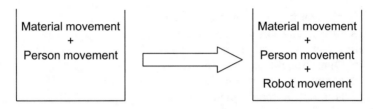

13 In many situations, various types of technologies and processes may coexist. Explain how this is because of different constraints and limitations such as:

(i) Different places in the plant where processes are carried out
(ii) Different quality requirements
(iii) Limitations on availability of appropriate equipment at all places simultaneously

14 In the context of forward logistics for new L.P.G. cylinders, mechanized equipment with a conveyor system and other modern technologies can be utilized for enhanced quality-level requirements related to operations such as painting. However, because of limitations on availability of such a system for the reverse logistics scenario concerning repair of used cylinders, an alternative process may be adopted at another place subject to meeting the desired quality levels. In such a situation, a low-cost arrangement may also be developed. Describe in detail a representation for this arrangement for painting the used cylinder as follows:

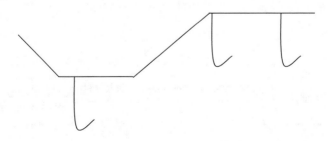

15 Elaborate what the reasons for relatively better service might be, such as:

   (i) After getting a message, the superiors anticipate the real cause of the problem and the associated remedy well. They select a well-qualified and experienced mechanic accordingly.

   (ii) It is ensured that the requisite tools are available with the person.

   (iii) The problem is sorted out in one go because of the desired expertise.

   (iv) There is better coordination and communication.

Also elaborate how this whole process can be automated with the help of technology.

16 Along with a system concerning real-time geographical location, truck drivers may also switch to computer-aided support while being behind the wheel. However, necessary skills need to be developed along with the desired training and orientation. Such skills may include:

   (i) Maintenance of the desired temperature for a certain category of items

   (ii) Time management related to arrival at the intended destination

   (iii) Coordination with other support services such as those related to the loading and unloading of items

17 Discuss the role of technology for providing a visionary approach.

18 What do you understand by the influence of infrastructure?

19 In a case in which a favourable infrastructure is available in a particular geographic location, how might it help in the following:

   (i) Installation, operation, and maintenance of appropriate facilities and technology

   (ii) Effective utilization of layout horizontally as well as vertically

   (iii) Easy approachability by the concerned parties such as suppliers, service providers, and customer representatives

20 With reference to the influence of infrastructure, narrate the following:

   (i) Location

   (ii) Layout

   (iii) Facilities and technology

   (iv) People

21 For technology development and adoption, narrate the following types of situations that may emerge:

   (i) The organization itself develops the technology

   (ii) The suppliers themselves develop the technology along with a negligible role of the buyer organization

   (iii) Both the organization and its supplier collaborate in developing the technology and related aspects

22 Discuss how people in general and employees of an organization in particular are more affected by the infrastructure in terms of good:

(i) Hospital/medical facilities
(ii) Educational institutes
(iii) Housing

23 In order to reduce the lead time regarding provision for housing, narrate why the collaborative plan, after inclusion of multiple objectives, should consider the following aspects:

(i) Whether procurement of land happens after getting the final booking
(ii) Whether procurement of land happens well in advance in anticipation
(iii) Whether project or construction activity should begin after the potential building or house gets booked
(iv) Whether the construction or project work should begin in anticipation of demands

24 What do you understand by the channel design?
25 Describe the aspects related to the conventional channel, such as:

(i) Input item suppliers
(ii) Design, procurement, and production
(iii) Logistics
(iv) Marketing and dealers/retailers
(v) Customer interface

26 Depending on the customer demand among other details, narrate how the whole supply chain design incorporates the following issues:

(i) How many suppliers are suitable: a few, many, or one?
(ii) Linking design according to customer orders and also procurement of input items and production of final product as per the demand/design
(iii) Number of warehouses and transportation planning
(iv) Dealer network, that is, how many dealers are suitable?
(v) Customer satisfaction approaches

27 As a promising approach towards channel design, elaborate how additional attention should be made to have holistic view with respect to:

(i) Linking location with layout
(ii) Linking layout with facility and technology
(iii) Appropriate combination of automation and human resources
(iv) Enabling infrastructure

28 Explain how the perfect linking in addition to conventional channel
    design is highly useful for overall satisfaction of all concerned such as:

    (i) Government
    (ii) Industry
    (iii) Channel partners
    (iv) Firms in collaboration/cooperation
    (v) Employees
    (vi) Society

BIBLIOGRAPHY

Boulaksil, Youssef and Jan C. Fransoo. Order release strategies to control outsourced operations in a supply chain. *International Journal of Production Economics*, Vol. 119, No. 1, 2009, 149–160.

Brown, Steve, John Bessant, and Fu Jia. *Strategic Operations Management*. Routledge, 2018.

Nahmias, S. *Production and Operations Analysis*. McGraw-Hill, 2001.

Sarker, B.R. and P.S. Babu. Effect of production cost on shelf life. *Int. J. Prod. Res.*, Vol. 31, No. 8, 1993, 1865–1872.

Sharma, Sanjay. Cycle time reduction in context to the make to order (MTO) environment. *Journal of Manufacturing Technology Management*, Vol. 24, No. 3, 2013, 448–464.

Sharma, Sanjay. Development of supplier relationship including cost of defectives in the cyclic production. *Production Planning & Control*, Vol. 24, No. 8–9, 2013, 759–768.

Sharma, Sanjay. Effects of an increase in manufacturing rate in the context of cyclic production. *International Journal of Advanced Manufacturing Technology*, Vol. 39, No. 7–8, 2008, 821–827.

Sharma, Sanjay. A fresh approach to performance evaluation in a multi-item production scenario. *European Journal of Operational Research*, Vol. 178, No. 2, 2007, 627–630.

Sharma, Sanjay. A modification for the carrying cost estimation with respect to the flexibility in production rate. *International Journal of Advanced Manufacturing Technology*, Vol. 36, No. 11–12, 2008, 1252–1260.

Sharma, Sanjay. On the flexibility of demand and production rate. *European Journal of Operational Research*, Vol. 190, No. 2, 2008, 557–561.

Sharma, Sanjay. Policies concerning decisions related to quality level. *International Journal of Production Economics*, Vol. 125, No. 1, 2010, 146–152.

Sharma, Sanjay. Theory of exchange. *European Journal of Operational Research*, Vol. 186, No. 1, 2008, 128–136.

Sharma, Sanjay. Towards a synergy between project and supply chain management. *International Journal of Industrial Engineering Computations*, Vol. 3, No. 5, 2012, 931–938.

Silver, E.A. Deliberately slowing down output in a family production context. *Int. J. Prod. Res.*, Vol. 28, No. 1, 1990, 17–27.

Smith, S.B. *Computer-Based Production and Inventory Control*. Prentice-Hall, 1989.

Tassabehji, Rana and Andrew Moorhouse. The changing role of procurement: Developing professional effectiveness. *Journal of Purchasing & Supply Management*, Vol. 14, No. 1, 2008, 55–68.

Williams, Christopher. *Management Consultancy for Innovation*. Routledge, 2019.

INDEX

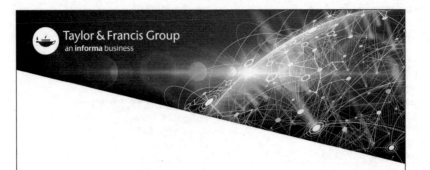